Sports- Biography

More Than Winning

More Than Winning

Tom Osborne
John E. Roberts

THOMAS NELSON PUBLISHERS
Nashville • Camden • New York

Published in Nashville, Tennessee, by Thomas Nelson, Inc. and distributed in Canada by Lawson Falle, Ltd., Cambridge, Ontario.

Printed in the United States of America.

ISBN 0-8407-5472-8

To the coaches and athletes of America, that their strivings, achievements, and responses will bring honor to the game and, even more, to their Creator.

Acknowledgments

The authors acknowledge with gratitude the support of their families, the tolerance of their employers, the assistance of their secretaries, the patience of the publisher, and the awesome grace of their Lord.

Contents

Foreword

When I was contacted by Thomas Nelson to write an autobiography, I had mixed feelings. Being a rather private person and not being too sure that my life story was appropriate material for a book, I had many reservations. On the other hand, I realize that we are living in a time when college athletics is under close scrutiny. There is a great deal of skepticism about the integrity of college athletics and much misunderstanding of what really goes on. Also I have been privileged to be associated with a football program and athletes and coaches that are of some interest to many people. Therefore, this book has been written in hopes that readers might gain a better understanding of college athletics in general and University of Nebraska football in particular. I don't think the overall picture in intercollegiate athletics today is as bleak as many would have us believe.

The book is a chronicle not only of events in my life but also is something of a record of my spiritual journey, a journey each of us is on. I hoped that this might be of some encouragement and interest to fellow travelers.

There are many people who deserve thanks and credit for the production of this book, most notably Bob Devaney, who gave me the opportunity to be a football coach. Also meriting appreciation are my fellow coaches at Nebraska, who have done so much to make our program what it is; the players, who have truly been an inspiration to me over the years and a source of great encouragement; my family, who have been very supportive; and especially, my wife Nancy, who has made great sacrifices in order for me to pursue a career in coaching and who has been an unfailing source of strength, comfort, and perspective throughout the years. I would also like to thank Jack Roberts for his expertise and his time in helping to make sure that this book came to fruition.

Whatever proceeds I receive from this book will go to religious and charitable organizations in an attempt to put back in some small way a part of what I have been given throughout my lifetime.

Preface

I first met the young head coach in 1974 in Washington, D.C., where we and others had gathered to discuss and lobby against some federal regulations that were being imposed on college athletics.

During the second day of hearings, the young coach sat with some of the elder statesmen of college football before a U.S. House of Representatives subcommittee, and he carried the ball into the senators' territory with comments that surprised everyone with their depth and eloquence.

I next encountered the coach after eight Big Eight football campaigns had seasoned him. He stood before a group of coaches at a Fellowship of Christian Athletes coaches' conference in Indiana and again carried the ball into this audience's territory, discussing from his heart both his successes and failures in life, and impressing everyone with his humility and sincerity.

Just a month later I met the coach again, and this occasion impressed me most. This time I was the speaker at an early morning coaches' breakfast in Lincoln, Nebraska, and he was at the door taking tickets with his hair messed up and looking as if he'd just climbed out of bed.

Nothing this coach has done—no victory he has coached, no championship he has secured, no award he has received—has revealed

7

more to me about the ingredients of his character than his effort as ticket-taker that early August morning. He's a humble servant.

He's also honest—uncompromisingly honest. So while it is customary for books like this to make up long-forgotten dialogue and fabricate details of situations the memory cannot recall, this one doesn't. It would betray the essence of the man.

At a time when characters receive more press than character, this man's story is a welcome change.

At a time when instability characterizes college sports, this man stands out. He's never coached anywhere but at the University of Nebraska, and, except for a few years when he was a professional football player, he's never lived more than a hundred miles from where he lives today.

It's been a pleasure to help Tom Osborne present his story in these pages. And even though he's never won fewer than nine games in any season as head coach, his story is about "More Than Winning."

John E. Roberts
Executive Vice President
Fellowship of Christian Athletes
August 1, 1985

Prologue

Coming Up
Short Again

January 2, 1984, Orange Bowl, Miami, Florida.
Fourth and eight at the Miami twenty-three yard line, trailing 31-24, less than a minute to play. I sensed that all of the seventy-two thousand fans in the stands and many of the millions watching on television were on their feet screaming. The chance to win the national championship that we had come so close to grasping the two previous years was now reduced to a few precious seconds and a short span of the chewed-up Orange Bowl turf.

I called a 41 sprint pass. This would give us a chance to hit our flanker, the speedy Irving Fryar, on a slant pass. If he was covered, our quarterback, Turner Gill, could pull the ball down and run the option to the outside.

I watched the play unfold. Turner started to his right down the line of scrimmage and raised his arm to throw the slant pass. The Miami left corner back and safety both moved toward Irving as he slanted toward mid-field. At the last instant, Turner pulled his arm down and ran toward the Miami defensive end. Just before they collided, Turner pitched the ball to our I-back, Jeff Smith. With the Miami secondary

9

chasing Irving, Jeff had running room to the outside. He got first down yardage easily and continued driving toward the goal line, encountering no opposition until he reached the three yard line, where he slammed into two defenders and dove across the goal line.

We had a chance. We were down 31-30 with forty seconds left in the game.

There was bedlam on our sideline. "Irving!" I shouted. I had spotted Irving Fryar, who had run off the field. "Tell Turner to run the two-pointer." I sent him back in with instructions to call the two-point play we had worked on in preparation for the game.

As our team huddled, the crowd noise was so loud that I could hear nothing else, but it was also so constant that I almost stopped noticing it. I was alone with my thoughts. People say that in moments of extreme danger they have had their whole lives pass through their minds. It was kind of like that for me—quick flashes of a life I'm going to tell you about in this book.

The team broke the huddle, moving away from me so I couldn't see the players' faces. I couldn't tell if there was confidence in their eyes or anxiety. *Darn!* I thought. *Biggest play of their careers and maybe mine, and down here on the sideline I have the worst view in the nation.*

Irving lined up in a slot formation to the right, Jeff Smith lined up in a wing position to the right of him, and our split end lined up outside both Jeff and Irving, giving us three receivers to the right side.

On the snap Irving drove toward the inside, taking with him the strong safety, who was playing him man-to-man. At the same time Jeff ran to the flat area vacated by Irving and our split end. Turner rolled to his right. "He's open!" someone yelled in my ear. The man trying to stay with Jeff was not going to be close enough to cover Jeff before he had caught the ball and sprinted the three yards to the end zone.

Turner released the ball into the night sky. The roar of the crowd crescendoed. And for an instant it looked as if we would connect and score. But the man covering Irving saw Jeff running to the outside, left Irving, and started for Jeff. He slipped slightly, then regained his balance and lunged desperately for the ball. He got two fingers on the ball and barely deflected it, causing it to bounce off Jeff's shoulder pads as he made a futile effort to turn and clutch it.

Some of the players on our sideline, who had twisted their bodies to help Jeff catch the ball, fell to the ground silently. A couple of them pounded the turf with their fists. A few others kicked at the ground or stomped around. I just closed my eyes, leaned over, and put my hands to my knees. When I opened my eyes, I saw the trampled ground and noticed my dirtied shoes and bright red slacks. Then I stood erect, began clapping, and welcomed our players back to the sideline with encouraging words.

It was a difficult moment, to say the least. The team that had won twelve straight games and had been ranked number one in the nation from the Kickoff Classic against Penn State in late August until the Orange Bowl game on January 2 had lost by one point. Some thought it was the finest college offensive squad of all time—a team with a Heisman Trophy winner in Mike Rozier, an Outland and Lombardi Trophy winner in Dean Steinkuhler, the number one NFL draft choice in Irving Fryar, a great quarterback in Turner Gill, and numerous other outstanding players. Yet there it was. Time had run out.

And the team that had gone 12-1 for two straight years had come up short again.

Chapter One

The Effect of Fine Persons

I felt I was prepared for it. Dad had suffered a heart attack fifteen years earlier—had arrived at a hospital in Massachusetts with no pulse before pulling through—so he had been living on borrowed time.

Still, when my brother, Jack, called February 13, 1984, there was the shock of sudden and irreplaceable loss. Jack said Dad had done a little snow shoveling, which he shouldn't have been doing (he was always doing things he shouldn't) and then got in the car and drove eight or nine blocks when he had a heart attack.

"He passed out," Jack said on the phone, "and his car slammed through the front door of a doctor's office. No one was hurt, but Dad never regained consciousness."

"A funeral," Dad often had said, "is not for the dead person but for the living." So Jack and I wanted the funeral to minister to the people who were there, as Dad would have wanted. We hoped people could enjoy themselves.

"We're grateful for the kind of person Dad has been and the many friends he's had," I told those gathered. "We're thankful he's had a full life. We're grateful for his sense of humor and for the joy we have in being with his friends."

As people left the church that raw, overcast winter day in Hastings, Nebraska, Jack and I greeted everyone and thanked each for coming. It was the kind of funeral Dad would have wanted to attend himself.

Dad's father, my grandfather, was named Tom Osborne. In his early teens he became very ill, and it was thought he might die. The common medication for his illness—a kind of fever—was whiskey, but he refused to drink it. He had made a pledge to never take "strong drink," and he stuck with that pledge almost at the cost of his life. He lost all of his hair and was very close to death. But he showed uncommon resolve—a trait he had in abundance, I am told.

He worked his way through Hastings College in the late 1890s, played football there, and then went into the ministry. He homesteaded some land in western Nebraska with the help of my grandmother. She lived on the land for several months with small children while he preached several hundred miles away in Wayne, Nebraska.

For most of his life he was a Presbyterian minister in the western Nebraska communities of Alliance, Bayard, Bridgeport, and Scottsbluff. He was killed when struck by lightning at the age of sixty-five. I was six years old at the time.

I've always looked up to and admired my grandfather more out of what I've heard about him than what I actually knew of him personally. As I remember, I was only with him three or four times. He had a dignified and erect way of moving and a sturdy build. He played tennis and liked to hunt. I greatly admired the fact that he was a minister and a man of conviction.

Yet he was a rugged person. Dad told me that once as a college student, my grandfather missed the stagecoach that traveled through Bayard and Alliance every three days, so he walked the forty-odd miles between the two towns.

Before entering the ministry, my grandfather was a cow-puncher. He spoke the Sioux Indian language well and was respected by the ranchers, early pioneers, and native Americans in western Nebraska. He was the person most often invited to officiate at funeral services of the early settlers, many of whom had never set foot inside a church door.

After several years in the ministry, he became active in politics and at one point was elected to the Nebraska state legislature. It is said that he once lost a close election because he refused to campaign. His thinking was that people knew him, and he didn't feel it was right to do anything to try to sway their opinion of whether or not to vote for him.

He had a large family and at times struggled financially. He developed throat trouble, lost his speaking voice, and couldn't preach for a period of years. So he had to turn to farming to support his wife and six children. During the years spent on the farm, my dad and his brother Clifford lived year-round in a tent. There wasn't room in the house for them.

My dad (his name was Charles) was influenced by being a preacher's kid. He reacted by trying to go out of his way at times to show that he wasn't overly pious. Sometimes he was a bit of a roughneck.

After graduation from Hastings College, where he played football like his father, he still hadn't had enough of the game, so he carried, in the trunk of his car, a football uniform he had "borrowed" from the college. As he traveled throughout Nebraska as a car salesman, he would convince high school coaches to let him scrimmage with their teams.

He also was quite a practical joker. One time while he was in college, he secretly visited the home of the dean late at night. The dean raised chickens, so my dad and a friend buried the chickens in the ground up to their necks along the path from the chicken coop to the house. In the morning there was quite a scene when the dean saw my dad's handiwork!

Dad took six years to get through Hastings College. He stayed out two years to work for his uncle, A. H. Jones, who owned an automobile dealership. The business began as a livery and moved into cars when they were introduced to Nebraskans. Dad continued in the business after graduation and eventually took over the enterprise, later transforming it into an irrigation business.

My maternal grandfather's parents had come from Ireland. Grandfather Welsh never finished high school. He moved into the St. Paul, Nebraska, area (about ninety miles west of Lincoln) in the 1920s and eventually became, for those days, a fairly wealthy man. He owned two farms and was doing well, but then he lost the farms in the Depression. He took a job in a St. Paul meat market and worked there until he retired. When I knew him, he was a meat-cutter, but he still had the weatherbeaten look of a man who had spent many years outdoors with crops and cattle.

For about five years during World War II, my Grandfather and Grandmother Welsh became like parents to me because my dad was fighting in Europe and my mother was working in a munitions plant and teaching school. My granddad would bring home each Saturday night after work a paycheck of something like forty-five dollars for the week. That seemed like an awful lot of money to me at the time.

On one occasion I was given fifty cents to go downtown on a Saturday night, and somehow I ended up playing in a vacant lot. There was a big sand pile, and I lost that fifty cents in it. I went back there repeatedly over the next several days and spent hours and hours looking for that fifty-cent piece. And how upset Mom was with me for losing that fifty cents! Of course, at that time, fifty cents was a *lot* of money.

I was born in February of 1937. Dad traveled as an automobile salesman during the first years of my life. He was home only on Saturday and Sunday nights and was gone again on Monday morning. As a result, my mom was lonely and, at times, a little anxious. She was home with me all the time, and she expected a great deal of me. My brother, Jack, was born when I was three. About that time she started teaching me to read and recite nursery rhymes. I think I could do some things in terms of recitation and memory that were a little unusual for a child my age because of the amount of time she spent with me.

I also was expected to carry a pretty good load around the house when Jack was born. I was treated more like an adult than a three-, four-, or five-year-old child is normally treated. In some ways this was good and in some ways probably bad. I learned a lot about being responsible, but I was never quite as much a child as I might have been.

Mom loved my brother and me very much and was an excellent mother. She also was an avid antique collector, and having two rambunctious sons was difficult for her because we spent a lot of time rough-housing and wrestling around the house.

Once when I was about four years old, Dad was home and he'd brought me a football. We were playing catch in the living room, where there was a curved glass dresser that was particularly important to Mom. Dad was sitting in front of this very valuable antique, and Mom was nervous about our playing catch there. But Dad kept assuring her, "There's nothing to worry about." Then for some reason I suddenly decided to kick the football. I don't know why, I just did it. I punted it over Dad's head into the curved glass of the precious antique. There was a tremendous crash, followed by tremendous misery!

I remember as vividly as any childhood memory the trauma of the next two or three days. Dad eventually went to one of the stores in town, and they were able to cast the curved glass in a separate mold. It was very expensive, but at least peace was restored in our household. I should have realized right then how disruptive football can be to family life!

Unlike many small Nebraska towns, St. Paul hasn't changed much since the 1940s. It's still quiet, patriotic, and conservative, with not much commerce. While I lived there during World War II, the big difference between me and most of the other kids I knew was that my dad was gone and theirs weren't. He really didn't have to go in the Army. He was thirty-seven, old enough that he would not have been drafted—but he enlisted after the Japanese attacked Pearl Harbor. I can still remember the report of the Pearl Harbor bombing coming over the radio. Dad jumped from his chair and said, "I'm going to get involved in that thing!" I was impressed with this, not realizing all it would mean in my life.

My mother—a slender, pretty redhead—was often preoccupied with Dad's being overseas. Sometimes we didn't hear from him for months at a time because of the poor communications during the war. There was one particularly difficult three-month interval during the Battle of the Bulge when we didn't receive any word from Dad.

Around this time I became rather resentful. Jack was about three and I was six or seven, and, of course, he was smaller. He also had a more sunny disposition, and I was more moody. As a result, he often received more attention and praise than I did. It was perceived that I was sometimes kind of rough on him, and my grandfather and grandmother often would side with him. A normal thing, of course, but I felt I wasn't appreciated very much or was some kind of bad person because I mistreated my brother or wasn't as helpful as I should have been.

There was a time when apparently I talked back to my Uncle Virgil, who lived across the street from us, and I got a pretty severe whipping from Mom. I was particularly upset about this because I felt I was unjustly accused. I really hadn't talked back to my uncle. It just seemed that I was on the "outs" with *everybody* in our family.

During those years in St. Paul, our play was stimulated by the war effort and was usually rough. I had two or three close friends, and we "battled" another group of neighborhood children who were a little older and were perceived as the "enemy." We had rock fights regularly, and on one such occasion I sustained a deep gash over one eye. One of my "best" days was when I hit one of the enemy in the back with a can filled with mud that had been baked hard to look like an artillery shell. This caused considerable pain, and the enemy left the scene limping badly.

On another occasion I threw a brick at the roof of an enemy house, but the brick fell short of the mark and went through a window. Mom found out about it and marched me to the enemy house, where I was forced to confess my misdeed to the enemy father. Much to my surprise and relief, he said he'd already fixed the window by stuffing a pillow in it and it was all right. I was amazed at this charitable attitude and redirected my attacks toward other enemy targets after that.

I went to high school football games regularly and can vividly recall playing "tackle the man who gets it" at half time out on the playing field. This game consisted of one person kicking the ball in the air and then about fifty boys chasing the person who caught the ball and tackling him, where upon the tackled person had to punt the ball away. My enthusiasm for this game was diminished considerably one night when about ten boys tackled me and smashed my face into the lime used to mark the field. I didn't think I would ever draw another normal breath.

During these years I often had nightmares and irrational fears, including a recurring nightmare in which German soldiers took over St. Paul and were marching down the street looking for me. The war took its toll even on those of us who weren't near the fighting.

The best memories of those war years are of wading in the warm waters of the Loup River fishing for catfish, days spent in a duck blind, and shooting my first rabbit with a German-made .22 rifle sent home by Dad.

Uncle Virgil, who looked then a lot like I do now (fairly tall, ruddy complexion, and red hair), was a very strong figure in my life at that time. He kind of took over for my dad. He was an avid hunter, fisherman, and trapper, and I accompanied him a lot on fishing and hunting trips. My great love for the outdoors and particularly for fishing was born during those years between ages six and ten. Fishing was probably the thing I looked forward to the most.

One time we had gone fishing and there was some grass that had grown out over the bank of the pond. Repeatedly, Virgil warned me I ought to be careful, that there was not a good, solid bank. Eventually, I got too close to the edge of the grass, stepped on it, and went down in the water. I remember going down and down in the pond. Dark, cold water poured over my head. My uncle turned around and saw just my hat floating on the surface, reached under my hat, and pulled me out. I'm sure there was absolutely no danger, but it was a frightening experience. I thought I was drowning.

Not having a father around meant I missed out on many events that involved fathers or complete families. Many times I had the feeling I was left out. That was another tough thing about the war.

My grandparents, having lost most of everything they had during the Depression, really valued a dollar. As a result, I absorbed the feeling that we were a little down and out, even though we really never lacked anything important.

My dad was almost a total stranger to me when he came back from the war. My memories of him when I was four years old and younger had been fleeting, and five years of separation is a long time to a young child. When he came back, I was ten years old, and I really didn't remember much about him. All I knew was what Mom had told me, what I'd envisioned his doing in the war, and what little I could learn of him in the letters he sent.

Part of me really wanted him back. Yet my life had developed along certain lines, and I knew he would disrupt things when he returned. I almost resented the fact he was going to uproot our familiar situation and inject himself again into our lives. I certainly had mixed feelings, and I felt guilty since I wasn't even sure I wanted him to come back.

Of course, a few months after he returned I got to know him better, and then I went into a period where I really idolized him. He would tell stories about things that happened in the war, things that happened when he played football in college, and events during the Depression. He was a great storyteller, and I deeply admired him and wanted to be like him. I grew very attached to him in the months and years after he got back; I didn't know how I ever got along without him.

He was a handsome, dark-haired man who was slightly above average height and tended to be a little overweight through middle age. He needed glasses because he read almost constantly.

I've always had great admiration for my dad, but the thing I admired most about him was the way he took care of Mom after she suffered a serious stroke in 1981. She wanted to stay at home. They had a woman who came during the day, but Dad stayed with Mom in the evenings and all day on Sunday. He cooked her meals and read to her. Even though he was in poor physical condition himself because of his heart attack in the fall of 1968, he got up with her once or twice every night. This was hard on him. It drained his strength from lack of sleep. Yet he wouldn't hear of any other arrangement. He was her main reason for living. They aged well and grew closer with the passage of time.

Someone has said, "The best effect of fine persons is felt after we have left their presence." Looking back at my childhood, I can see there were strong role models in my Grandfather Osborne, my dad, and my Uncle Virgil. There were the care and unwavering love and trust of my mom and my Grandmother Welsh. Yet there was also an insecurity—a feeling at times of being from the wrong side of the tracks which resulted from the absence of my father and the uncertainty of wartime.

Much of my life has been directed toward proving something—what it is I really don't know—but the roots of that striving, I am sure, lie in the events surrounding my childhood experiences during World War II.

Chapter Two

Growing Up

I wanted to be an athlete very much. Athletics for me, as for many kids then and now, was my god—the most important thing in my life for a while.

I had been fairly successful in playground games at the grade school in St. Paul, but my interest in athletics really intensified when my father came back from World War II. He took me to games, played catch, and talked to me about athletics. Then we moved forty miles south to Hastings, Nebraska, across the street from Hastings College where my Grandfather Osborne had played on the school's first football teams and Dad had played some thirty years later.

I was at the college to watch practice practically every night during football season. My friends and I played pick-up games on the college lawns. In fact, on several occasions, the president of the college ran us off the campus because we were wearing out the grass.

During basketball season we all hung around the college gym after practice to shoot baskets until they turned out the lights. We often even shot at one end of the court while the team practiced at the other. Whenever the players came our way we scampered off the court. When the action headed back toward the other basket, we hovered around "our" basket again—and got in a short scrimmage until the players headed our way again.

I didn't play organized football until the eighth grade. Then I didn't get to play too much in the first game. I was really burned up, but the coach put me in the second game and I did pretty well. I went on to play a lot the rest of the season.

In junior high basketball I played well because I was fairly tall. But one time one of the coaches told me, "You'll never be any good until you're willing to get your face scratched up." He was saying that I shot the ball pretty well but remained aloof from any kind of contact, rebounding, or the other really tough things in basketball. His remark made me angry, but from that point on I became a very aggressive basketball player. I guess his talking to me that way served a purpose. Maybe it got the best out of me. I don't use that technique with college athletes, however, because I'm not very good at it and it's as often counterproductive as it is effective.

By the ninth grade I was a successful athlete. I was a good hurdler and was capable in basketball and football. As a result of my success, I had a fairly high opinion of myself. I didn't see myself as cocky, but apparently some of the older players in high school did.

During the summer between the ninth and tenth grades, I got involved in Junior Legion baseball and participated for the first time with players who were two and three years older than I was. I really got my ears pinned back.

I had become a fairly friendly, talkative guy—at least *I* thought I was friendly. The players thought I was just too talkative and started calling me "Yak," sometimes not in a very kind way. I resented this. I hadn't thought of myself as being a yakker, but they saw me that way.

I hoped very much I would be able to play a lot or start on that baseball team, but there were probably fourteen or fifteen of us on the team and I sat on the bench the whole summer. It was my first extended time as a bench warmer, and I didn't take it well. I was very frustrated. I was at bat only twenty-four or twenty-five times and only got one or two hits. It was the first failure I had experienced in athletics, even though I was on a very good team.

Because I was frustrated with not playing as much or as well as I had wanted, and was overly sensitive to the razzing I was getting from some of the older players, I crawled into a shell. I decided that rather than opening up and expressing myself as I had earlier in the summer, I wasn't going to take the chance of being vulnerable again. So I withdrew and didn't talk much around those guys, and this developed into a general pattern of being reticent, of keeping things inside myself.

This served me well as an athlete, because the emotions and sometimes hostilities I had pent up inside gave me tremendous drive and incentive to play well. At the same time I developed some unhealthy emotional patterns in not really talking about my feelings, expressing neither anger nor joy. I was a very quiet and somewhat withdrawn person during the rest of my high school career, and I trace much of it to that experience in the summer between my ninth and tenth grade years.

I didn't handle that situation well. I was thrown in with a group of older players who were probably well-intentioned and justified in putting me in my place, but they did so more thoroughly than they may ever have intended.

Things went better in the fall when football started. Football was always my favorite sport, and I became the second-string quarterback as a sophomore. I played a good deal and even started a game or two toward the end of the season. This was somewhat remarkable because of my size. I was 6'2" and weighed 135 pounds, a real string bean.

We had a senior fullback named Duck Daugherty who was also 6'2" but who weighed 60 pounds more than I. He was a tough fellow who later played at Oklahoma A & M. The second team always scrimmaged the first team, and I played safety on the second team when the first team had the ball. Duck ran over me two or three times every scrimmage. I don't think I brought him down once all year.

Just before the start of my junior year of high school—the summer of 1953—we won the state baseball tournament and did well at the regional tournament, too.

Although I was a good third baseman, I made two straight errors on ground balls in the state championship game and got a real chewing out from our coach, Earl Applebee. I handled nine more chances that night without an error but was really steaming. I just didn't handle criticism well. Earl was a tough coach and I often resented his discipline, but later I grew to appreciate him and we became very good friends.

That fall I was the starting quarterback on the high school football team. We ended up ranked second or third in the state. We lost only one game by one point late in the season to arch rival Grand Island. The weather that night was mild and there were about six thousand people there, filling the bleachers and surrounding the field.

In the last couple of minutes I made a run of forty yards and was down—or nearly down—on one knee when another tackler barreled into me and I lost the ball. The officials ruled it a fumble, and that ended our last scoring attempt. We ended up losing 21-20. I remember feeling very bad about losing but also being proud of the team and the way we had played, because Grand Island had a great football team.

That winter our team won the 1954 state high school basketball tournament. It was the only time in many years, either before or since, that Hastings won the state basketball title. I was a junior, and the other starters were seniors. I was 6'3" plus and played guard. Our forwards and centers were 6'5", and the other guard was 6'2". That was a pretty big high school basketball team in those days.

In my senior year I had a very good football season. We were 6-3, losing a couple of very close ballgames. I played quarterback, safety, and ran back punts and kick-offs. I was second team all-state quarterback behind Mike Dugan from Omaha, who went on to Notre Dame.

I also made the all-state team in basketball that year. We had a good team but were beaten out in a very close game in the district playoffs by the team that eventually won the state championship.

Then in track I got second place in the state meet in the 440-yard dash. I won the discus, which I had just started throwing that spring, by a half-inch margin.

At the end of that school year, I was named "High School Athlete of the Year" in Nebraska. This honor was mostly because I did a lot of things well. I wasn't a particularly great athlete in any one sport, but I did participate in four sports and our teams had done reasonably well.

I learned about the award when some reporter from the *Omaha World Herald* came out and took some pictures. That's all there was to it. I thought it was a nice honor, and yet I was a little bit uncomfortable with it because I felt some people in Hastings—my friends—might resent it, thinking I was stuck up and the like. Still, I appreciated it.

My recruitment by colleges wasn't anything like what athletes to-day experience. I was offered separate scholarships in football and basketball at the University of Nebraska, but my recruitment merely consisted of getting one or two letters from the football and basketball coaches, just asking me to come down for an all-sports day, when the spring football game was played along with a baseball game and track meet.

I went to see the football coach that day in his office. "How would you like to be a Nebraska football player?" he asked without formality.

"I'd certainly think about it."

He said, "Well, if you want to come, you've got a scholarship."

"That's nice," I said, and left.

There was none of the extensive recruiting effort I've seen and done. I don't believe he ever came out to see me or even called me on the phone. I had the feeling it was sort of a take-it-or-leave-it proposition and that they weren't all that interested in me.

Years later, after I became a coach at Nebraska, the trainer, Paul Schneider, told me that the coaches at that time had told him I was one of the players in the state they were most interested in. I found it a little hard to believe in view of the meager efforts they made to recruit me. Many of the coaches at the University at that time were native Pennsylvanians, and they did a lot of recruiting in and around Pennsylvania. Maybe they didn't think very much of Nebraska high school football. I don't know. It's sure been good to me!

My recruitment in basketball was much the same. The coach looked me up at the state track meet, which was held on the University of Nebraska campus, and asked if I wanted to play basketball. He said I would be given a scholarship if I wanted it. I told him I was really interested in playing both football and basketball, but he strongly discouraged me from doing both. He said he didn't think I could do both very well (and I'm sure he was right). Again, there was no phone call and no personal visit.

Maybe those coaches were a little low-key in their recruiting, but I've seen plenty of the other extreme where there's been too much doting over a high school athlete, which sometimes results in strange occurrences.

For example, seven or eight years ago a quarterback in the Dallas area had committed verbally to attend Nebraska. In the South a commitment is usually pretty strong. There's more or less an unwritten code that if you make a verbal commitment, it's almost like something signed in blood.

This player told us he was definitely coming to Nebraska. At that time the head coach could be present at the signing of a player, and I advised him I'd be there. So I traveled to Dallas the night before the signing date. I went to his house and sat in his living room for about three hours and talked to him and his parents. We discussed the signing procedure and all kinds of questions about the courses he was going to take at school, spring football, and so forth. There was absolutely no question or any hint of difficulty. I told them I was going to stay at a motel and gave them the number in case they had any other questions.

The agreement was that I would meet them at the school in the morning at 8:00. So I was there about 7:45. I sat there and talked to the coach, who was very much pro-Nebraska. Eight o'clock came and went. Then 8:15 and he still wasn't there. About 8:30 he showed up. By now there were seven or eight high school assistant coaches sitting around in the coach's office. The player came in and said, "Coach, I have signed with Southern Methodist University."

I laughed. Everybody laughed. "Sure you have," we said.

He said, "No, I really did. I signed with SMU this morning."

Finally, after about five minutes, we got it through our heads that he really *had* signed with SMU. Every one of the assistant coaches got up and stomped out because they all thought he was committed to Nebraska. The poor head coach turned white—as if somebody had shot him. It was one of the most unbelievable things I'd ever been involved in because of the absolute certainty that he would sign with Nebraska.

I found out later the player's mother had not wanted him to play far from home and had arranged the whole thing. The player's father didn't know his son hadn't signed with Nebraska until he arrived home from work that night.

Another time I was involved in recruiting a linebacker in Kansas City. He had signed a Big Eight letter-of-intent, which at that time came out a week ahead of the national letter. When he signed the Big

Eight letter, he publicly acknowledged he was going to Nebraska. That's what he told us. It was a firm commitment that had even been reported in Kansas City newspapers.

Our defensive coordinator, Charlie McBride, and I went down there the day before the national signing date and had a little trouble finding him. We got to be a little suspicious about it and finally realized the University of Texas was still in the picture. When we went over to school the morning of the signing, he said he was still waiting to make up his mind. We were supposed to come over to his house at 2:00 that afternoon.

So we showed up at his house. There were a lot of cars in front, and it turned out his high school coach was there, along with a couple of teachers, his mother, and a couple of his mother's friends. Also sitting in the living room was Texas head coach Fred Akers and an assistant.

We sat there and talked for a while. The player went in the other room and talked to his high school coach, his junior high principal, and some other people. He came back in and looked at Fred and me, and then walked back in the other room and had another conversation. This went on for about a half hour. He walked in and out maybe five times. His mother was getting very nervous. And of course Fred and I were getting a little upset because this was the signing date, and we were sitting there in one living room when we should have been three or four places. But there we sat, spinning our wheels.

Finally the player came in the living room, looked at me, and smiled. I began to feel relieved. Then he said, "Well, I'm gonna go to Texas."

One of the friends of his mother started shrieking. She went over and collapsed in the corner. His mother looked shocked. She had wanted him to go to Nebraska. She'd never met Fred Akers before that day. It seemed as though everybody had chosen sides and they were either cheering or crying. It was the doggonedest scene I'd ever witnessed, and certainly one of the strangest recruiting situations I've ever been in.

Well, there was certainly no doting over me. In addition to Nebraska, the University of Wyoming, Denver University, and one or two smaller schools offered me scholarships, but it was mostly through the mail. No pressure. No visits.

Ironically, one school whose football program I really admired at that time was the University of Oklahoma. They'd finished in the top ten every year I was playing high school football, and I think had they offered me a scholarship I would have been excited and very interested. But I didn't hear from them. I can't imagine how different my life might have been if Oklahoma had been interested in me.

I had grown up across the street from Hastings College, a private church-related school. When I was in grade school and junior high, I rarely missed a Hastings College football or basketball practice and never missed a game. In high school, I spent many of my weekends on the college's practice fields or in its gym.

Often young people feel they're making a particular decision, only to realize later the subtle pressure parents used to influence their choices. But I really felt then that I made the decision, and I can still say I never felt pressure from my parents to attend Hastings College. My familiarity with the town, the school, and the coaches was a major factor in choosing Hastings. I was also concerned with the social life at larger schools—I wasn't into the drinking scene—and I thought I wouldn't be bothered with that at Hastings, that I would be freer to choose what I wanted to do socially.

The Hastings College football coach, Tom McLaughlin, was a good personal friend of mine, and he proposed the idea that if I went to Hastings I could play both football and basketball. It was in late May or June that I finally told Coach McLaughlin I was going to go to Hastings, with the idea I would try to participate in football, basketball, and track. Tom told me I could have a scholarship if I wanted it, but his money was limited and he would appreciate it if I paid my own way. He pointed out that I could live at home, and he would help me obtain summer employment. So I put myself through school and played three sports. I believe that this experience helped me appreciate what our walk-ons go through here at Nebraska.

Chapter Three

Discovered in the Mineral Water Bowl

Kearney State had a winning streak of some twenty straight coming into the game against us in my junior year, 1957, at Hastings College. It was a cold, clear night late in the season. The field was fast and there was a "standing room only" crowd—about five thousand people.

Kearney was heavily favored. They were our nearest and greatest rival and had around four thousand students, while Hastings had only eight hundred. The Kearney football team had a lot more players too. They usually had about one hundred and fifty players out for football, and Hastings had around sixty. We didn't have much depth, maybe thirteen or fourteen players who could be counted on to do well in a tough game.

But we went out and played very well that evening and were ahead 26-0 at the half. We played single platoon football (one team playing both offense and defense), but Kearney rotated three teams. At the half I was exhausted and wondered if we could hang on. We did, fortunately, and ended up winning the game 26-6. It was a tremendous victory.

We had an undefeated team that year and played in the Mineral Water Bowl in Excelsior Springs, Missouri, twenty miles northeast of Kansas City. But we were beaten badly in the game by William Jewell College of nearby Liberty, Missouri. They ran the single wing, and from my safety position I had to make at least a dozen tackles. I had never seen such holes open up. Our team had never played against anything like it. Spinners. Buck laterals. Trapping. We were confused, and I got beaten to a pulp.

I was the all-conference quarterback that year, as well as in my sophomore and senior years, and I was all-conference in basketball that year and my sophomore year too. We had fine basketball teams. We won the conference championship my freshman, sophomore, and junior years and had two appearances in the NAIA national tournament.

During my junior season of basketball I developed a sideache that wouldn't go away. A doctor diagnosed it as appendicitis and decided to operate immediately. I told him I didn't want to miss any basketball games, so, being young and innovative, this doctor cross-stitched me in such a way that he thought I could play sooner. I practiced four days later and two days after that played against Kearney—not very well, but I played.

After the game the doctor informed that he went to the game to see me play and that he hadn't realized until then how much physical contact there was in college basketball. He gave me the clear impression that he wouldn't have made the same decision if he had it to do over again. "I had visions," he said, "of having to go down on the court and restitch your right side during the game."

My senior year was a disappointment. I received a few injuries in football—an injured elbow, calcium in both thighs—and my play in both football and basketball was affected.

We seemed to develop friction on the basketball team my senior year, too. We didn't have as good a team attitude as we normally had, and I felt there was a certain amount of resentment toward me. Maybe it was because I had received a lot of publicity. I had been selected "College Athlete of the Year" in Nebraska after my junior year.

The attention was not something I had solicited. In fact, I didn't particularly enjoy or want it. I was uncomfortable with some of it. I could understand my teammates' resenting it, and yet I was really frustrated by the situation because I felt it affected our play. We had a winning season, but it *felt* nothing like the year before.

Jack, my brother, had enrolled at Hastings and was a freshman my senior year. I had filled out some since high school, but Jack was pretty skinny at 6'0" and 160 pounds. We both made sharp contrasts to Tom McLaughlin, our football and track coach, who had a blocky-looking body and thin, sandy hair. Tom used a hearing aid and became quite adept at hearing only what he wanted to hear.

Having Jack on the football and track teams helped make up for some of the disappointments of that senior year. Jack matured late and eventually became a good football player and an outstanding track man. He held numerous records in the hurdles, long jump, and triple jump.

Of all the things I did in athletics, the only thing I never really enjoyed was the 440-yard dash. I loved the hurdles but tore a muscle sheath so badly in high school that I never was able to hurdle after my junior year. As a result, I was moved to the quarter mile my senior year and hated every race. I had a good, long stride, won most of the time, and was eventually able to run it in forty-nine seconds, but it always hurt physically and mentally.

I can recall one meet in college that was held only a few days after our last basketball game in March. It was cold, and light snow was falling. I wasn't in shape for track, but Tom McLaughlin talked me into running because we "needed the points." Tom was good at talking me into things. Well, I ran, and I think I won. But I have never been so sick in my life. I literally couldn't get up off the ground for over an hour and spent the next two hours re-examining my lunch.

Nothing points out better the compulsive way in which I approached athletics than the fact that I continued to run this crazy race for four years of college without ever really being able to adequately prepare for it and without ever enjoying it. I suppose my philosophy was, "If it hurts, it must be good for you." You can imagine what I thought of the slogan, "If it feels good, do it" that was so frequently declared in the late sixties and seventies.

Hastings was (and still is) a lovely town. "Neat" describes it best.

No heavy industry. A college town where houses and lawns are well-kept.

We lived in a white, three-bedroom frame house only two blocks from the predominantly red-brick buildings of the college campus, which was very compact—just three or four blocks square. I could walk across the campus in two or three minutes, and it's no bigger today.

I was a little out of the mainstream of college life. I didn't have an athletic scholarship so I lived at home, ate my meals at home, did my studying at home, and worked in the summer to try to pay my way through school. As a result, my social life was limited.

I dated a lot, had two or three different girlfriends, even became engaged for a while to a girl I dated at the college. So it wasn't as if I were a recluse. But because I didn't live in one of the dorms and didn't eat regularly at the college dining hall, I felt many times that I wasn't quite as much a part of college life as many other students.

Of course, my athletic experience led to a wide circle of acquaintances. I think I knew most all of the eight hundred students at Hastings College and as well-acquainted with the faculty. What I appreciated most about the college was the faculty. Because they were there first to teach, not to do research or make names for themselves, they were accessible to students and friendly, and they worked hard at their classroom preparation.

Hastings provided a very good experience for me. It was the kind of school where a person could sample lots of different academic disciplines. I enjoyed English and psychology courses, majored in history, took a minor in political science, had some accounting and business, took one or two education courses, and also enjoyed math classes and courses in humanities, besides taking a foreign language. I came out of Hastings with a broad, general education. It was a comfortable and rich academic environment.

In contrast, the experience our players have at the University of Nebraska is more specialized both on and off the field. They do things very well but are not able to sample as many sports, activities, or academic pursuits. At Hastings, I never lifted a weight, never threw the ball any more than just a couple of weeks before the season started, and never really was able to specialize in any one thing. I guess that's the way my academics were, too. I sampled a lot of different disciplines and wasn't nearly as focused in one area as many university students are today. I received a fine education but wasn't as well prepared to work in a specific field as most of our Nebraska players are. I majored in history and my grade-point average at Hastings was 3.8. I was given the Bronco Award at the conclusion of my senior year—an award that is given for over-all contribution to the college.

Ironically, the battering I took playing in the Mineral Bowl led to my chance to pay professional football. John Waldorf, who later became the commissioner of officials of the Big Eight Conference, was officiating the game, and his brother Lynn "Pappy" Waldorf was the director of personnel for the San Francisco 49ers. John told Lynn about me, and the 49ers evidently kept me in their files. I was drafted in the eighteenth round after my senior year.

There were only twelve professional football teams then as opposed to the twenty-eight in the National Football League today, plus the United States Football League. So there was probably more talent for each team when I was drafted. And while an eighteenth round draft choice wasn't very high, it is still one of the finer honors I've had, coming out of a small college like Hastings. I don't believe there have been any other players who have made professional football teams from Hastings. I'm sure many fine players never got a chance, so I feel very fortunate to have been "discovered."

All things considered, Hastings College was a very good experience and helped provide me with tools and skills that would prove to be very helpful with the passage of time.

Chapter Four

Survival

When I arrived at the 49ers' training camp in 1959, there were exactly thirty-six returning veterans and thirty-six spots on the roster (as compared to forty-five players carried by professional teams today). Competing for those jobs were something like seventy or eighty rookies. It looked bleak for a young man from Hastings.

I had been a quarterback in college, but after a day or two of practice, head coach Red Hickey called me into his office. It was the first time I had been alone and face-to-face with Red, whose thinning hair and florid face suited his name well. He was a big man (6'1", 220 pounds) and had a disposition that was alternatingly affable and stern, but sometimes punctuated with an explosive temper.

"Tom," he said, "we've got two quarterbacks—Brodie and Tittle—and we're only going to keep two. If you think you can beat one of 'em out, go ahead and try. If not, I'd be glad to try you at another position."

Y. A. Tittle and John Brodie were both veterans, so I assumed there was no possibility of making it at quarterback. I became closer to John than Y. A., by the way, because John had been in the National Football League only a couple of years and was more my age. I guess as second team quarterback he related better to someone struggling to make the team.

Y. A. was certainly not unfriendly, but at that time he was an eleven- or twelve-year veteran who had seen it all, done it all. Already bald, he was an established star and more aloof.

Anyway, I told Red I would be a receiver instead of a quarterback. But they had five great veteran receivers, too—Billy Wilson, R. C. Owens, Clyde Conner, Fred Dougan, and Hugh McElhanny, who was moved to receiver from running back. I survived to the last cut, when they told me they would like to keep me on the taxi squad for a year. I told them I would go to seminary instead. They gave me the toughest line in negotiations. They said, "That will be fine."

I had been urged by a registrar at Hastings College to apply for a Rockefeller grant, and I also applied for a Rhodes Scholarship. I wasn't selected for the Rhodes honor, but was given a Rockefeller grant for a year of study at a seminary. The idea behind the Rockefeller grant was to get people into seminary who didn't know for sure if they wanted to enter the ministry. It simply provided a year of exposure to seminary study. Since I won the scholarship, I decided I would take it.

The 49ers' regular-season practice facility was in Redwood City, which was thirty or forty miles south of San Francisco. So I chose San Anselmo Seminary, a Presbyterian institution north of San Francisco. It was the closest seminary I could find to the 49ers' workouts.

I went to school, but I just kept missing football. I wasn't sure I was cut out to be a minister and wasn't sure I even wanted to go to seminary that badly. So after two weeks I told the people at the seminary I was going to go back and try to play professional football.

I rejoined the 49ers. I was one of four or five players put on their taxi squad. This gave me an opportunity to practice every day with the team, improve myself, and learn the 49er system in case someone got hurt at my position. I couldn't suit up for the games, but I traveled with the team on long road trips to places like Chicago and Detroit, and we were gone for a couple of weeks at a time.

Another on the taxi squad was Jack Kemp, now a U.S. Congressman. We became good friends and roomed together on a couple of road trips. He was not the stereotypical football player. He was quite intellectual and often got chided for his reading. His studiousness was a great influence on me.

Jack had been around the league two or three years by that time. He had spent a year with the Detroit Lions, been in Canada for a year, been released up there, and bounced around a bit more. Eventually the start of the American Football League gave him a chance to try out with the Chargers, which eventually opened the door for his great career in Buffalo. I remember being with Jack the night "Fido" Murphy signed him with the Chargers. Fido offered me a contract, too, but I had my heart set on being a 49er and turned it down.

I really stood in awe of the 49ers because I had come from a very small school and had read about people like Joe Perry, Hugh McElhanny, Y. A. Tittle, and Billy Wilson for years. All of a sudden there I was playing with them! Or at least *practicing* with them.

It didn't seem at first as though I had any right to be on the same football field. But as time went on I began to realize football was football, they were as human as I was, and I could be competitive. I worked very hard.

I developed a really bad ear infection on the way out to the 49er camp and practiced the first two or three weeks of training camp with a fever and both ears swollen shut at times. Eventually the team doctor got the infection under control, but not until he had given me two or three shots of penicillin.

The 49er pre-season training camp was held at St. Mary's College in Moraga, California, which is about thirty miles to the east of Oakland. While the weather down in the Bay area might be in the fifties and sixties, Moraga was up through a tunnel on the other side of a range of hills where the weather was always much hotter. Pre-season was grueling because we went through five or six weeks of two-a-day practices in weather where many days the temperature was $90°-100°$.

It seemed like a lot of professional football was endurance. Survival. If you could avoid getting hurt, stay around, and keep working, you had a chance. So many players eliminated themselves by quitting or getting hurt.

I recall one night that Dan James, the 49ers' number one draft choice, told me he'd had enough and was going home to Ohio. I put him on the bus, and Dan left me his playbook and also the dubious privilege of informing Red Hickey that his number one draft choice had gone home. I found out first-hand that Red had quite a temper.

When I went out west for training camp, I had felt there was almost no chance I would make the team, but day after day of practice went by and I would still be there. We played exhibition games and I would still be there. I was really fortunate, I guess, to even make the taxi squad.

What I remember most about professional football was not the glamorous stuff. It was the training camps! They were interminably long. The physical demand was very great, practicing twice a day for as many as six weeks. But worse was the mental strain, the pressure to do well every day to make sure you made the team. I felt I was always in a position of being disposed of, especially because I was not a great athlete or a high draft choice. But I hung on all season.

The players were an interesting lot. One of our defensive linemen liked to hunt deer, and he slipped out after bed check to hunt in the hills around St. Mary's. One night he ran into a fence and severely lacerated a delicate part of his anatomy. He knew he needed the wound sewed up, but he couldn't let Red know he was out late, and he didn't trust the team doctor. So he woke up the trainer and had him sew him up on the training table without any anesthetic. He practiced the next day and Red never found out about it.

Then there was Bob St. Clair, 6'9" and 270 pounds, who ate his steaks raw, not even singed. My roommate was a very overweight tackle from College of Puget Sound. He informed me one night that he would never get cut "because the coaches like to watch me work." The next morning he was gone. Needless to say, then as now the most interesting thing about the game was the athletes.

After the season I spent six months in the Army reserve down at Fort Ord in California—two months learning how to shoot and fight, then four months sitting and typing. Afterward I went back to the 49ers, went through camp again, and played in most of the exhibition games. I thought I played fairly well, but the 49ers had signed Ray Norton, a sprinter from the Olympics. He had great speed and they were trying to make a player out of him, so they released me. I was picked up almost the same day, however, by the Washington Redskins.

It was kind of a strange feeling getting on an airplane, flying across country, and going from an NFL taxi squad to the real thing. All of a sudden I had made the NFL. It was an exciting time!

It was also a little bit of a struggle, because I had gotten familiar with the 49er players and their system. Now I was with the Redskins, who were getting ready in a period of three or four days to start their first regular season game.

The Redskins were not a very good football team, not nearly as talented at that time as the 49ers. I played sparingly that first year behind Joe Walton, catching only ten or eleven passes. But I enjoyed the experience. I felt as the season went on that I could be a starter, possibly deserved to be a starter, but I was just used as a slot player.

After the season I went back to California and attended graduate school at the University of Southern California. Actually, I had thought about attending George Washington University School of Law in Washington, D.C., but I had left my car with a girl to whom I was engaged in California and thought I needed first to see where that relationship was going, and second, to get the car. She had attended Hastings College but now was teaching school in Santa Maria, so USC was the closest place to her for me to do graduate work in another subject in which I had an interest, psychology. I lived in USC's freshman athletic dorm and rode herd on the players, people such as Willie Brown, Craig Beathard, and Hal Bedsole. I had asked John McKay for a coaching job, but he said he didn't need any graduate assistants, just someone to live in the athletic dorm as a counselor. So I did that and took twelve hours of graduate courses in psychology at USC. When the semester ended, so did the engagement.

The next year, 1961, I went back to the Redskins. Joe Walton had been traded to the New York Giants, so I had a chance to be the starter at flanker.

My season got off to a poor start, however: I pulled a hamstring slightly on the first day of practice. They put us through a mile run which I ran pretty fast, maybe faster than I should have. That was followed by forty-yard dashes. I think I tightened up a little in the mile run and pulled the hamstring in the races. I was able to continue to play with the injury. It was not a complete tear, just a very sore leg.

Every week, as time went on, they injected the leg with Novocain the day of the game, and I was able to get through it. But I didn't feel I was functioning at 100 percent. Usually I couldn't practice much on

Monday or Tuesday. By Wednesday I was able to at least get through the plays. By Sunday I was recovered enough that I could play again. But, in the process, I did a lot of damage to the hamstring, particularly with all the injections I took.

The last exhibition game of the pre-season that year was a crucial time for me. We were playing the Green Bay Packers, coached by Vince Lombardi, in Columbus, Georgia. The temperature, even at night, was over 90°, and the humidity was also over 90 percent. It was one of those times when you knew you had better play well or you would be released, as by that time only good players were left on the squad and competition was fierce.

I recall the trainer or doctor coming around with a bottle of pills. He indicated the pills would give us greater energy and endurance. They weren't illegal, but people were naive about them. One of our players had passed out after taking eight or nine pills, so I was leery of them. But on this day—it was hot, I knew I would play a lot, and I knew I had to play well to stick with the team—I took one.

Whether the pill helped or not I don't know, but I did catch four passes including one for a touchdown and, in general, had a good game. I knew I had made the team. I also knew I wasn't taking any more pills, as I was still wide awake at 4:00 A.M. and my heart was working overtime. At that time there wasn't much general knowledge about stimulants, but I didn't need to read a book to decide that "speed" was dangerous and I wanted no part of it.

At Nebraska, we've recently initiated a random drug testing program with our squad for steroids and "street" drugs such as marijuana, cocaine, and "speed." The results have been gratifying in that we have found little drug abuse, and the players and their parents have accepted the testing well.

If a player tests positive once, he is made to enroll in a drug education course and is monitored weekly until his system is clear. A letter is sent to his parents explaining his difficulty, and he is put on probation. If he is caught with drugs in his system a second time, he is suspended from the team. In the first year of the testing, we had four or five players test positively. We believe that this indicates a relatively light drug problem among our players.

Steroids are difficult to detect. Recent publicity about heart, liver, and kidney damage because of steroid use by athletes has served as a deterrent. We have turned up very little steroid use in our testing to this date, although this continues to be a concern.

However, the major drug problem in the United States as a whole today, from grade school through retirement age, is alcohol abuse. Alcohol is almost impossible to test for because it leaves the system so rapidly. It may sound archaic, but I encourage our players toward total abstinence. Hopefully, this encouragement doesn't fall on deaf ears, and I don't believe it does.

At the end of my third year of professional football, I was pretty well convinced that, with all the scarring my hamstring had undergone, I would not be able to go back and make the team another year. The injury had diminished my speed a good deal. Also, I had become disenchanted with some things about the Redskins.

For instance, they had taken the exhibition money out of our contract, which was a violation of NFL rules. At that time each player was paid something like $100 for each of the five exhibition games, and then the value of the contract for the remaining twelve games of the season was supposed to be over and above the exhibition money. However, the Redskins deducted the $500 from the value of our contract. That may seem like a minor amount, but I believe my first contract was for $6,500 and my last one was for $8,500. Therefore, $500 represented a fair amount of the total contract, and the players protested this decision. We pointed out to the Redskins' management that it was a violation of league rules, and they assured us they would send the money after the season.

Well, I contacted them two or three more times, and they never did send the money. So I went back to the University of Nebraska to go to graduate school and embarked on a course of study in educational psychology. It was a last-minute decision, but I knew a student in that program at Nebraska wo seemed to like the school. And since Nebraska was home, it made sense to continue there the course of study I had started at U.S.C. I got a job as a graduate assistant football coach at Nebraska and, within a couple of months of enrolling, met my wife-to-be, Nancy.

Because of a combination of things—injuries, the instability of professional football, the contract dispute—I decided I wasn't going to return.

I think the Redskins assumed I *would* come back, however, because they seemed surprised when I informed them otherwise. They even offered to send me the $500!

I had ended the season with twenty-two or twenty-three receptions and was the second leading receiver on the team, despite playing subpar because of the hamstring injury. I thought I had played fairly well, generally up to NFL standards at the time.

That year in pro football was important to me in that the one thing going to Hastings College had always left me with was a little doubt about what level of football I could have competed on. Even though I'd been successful at Hastings, I still wondered at times if I could have played major college football. The ability to hang on in the NFL, and eventually play and even start, removed that doubt in my mind and was gratifying.

I enjoyed my relationship with the players in the NFL. I really admired and respected many of the coaches I met. Some I didn't. The total importance attached to winning in professional football was unattractive to me. That's why I've never been too interested in leaving college football for pro football. The pressure to win at the college level is intense enough.

Chapter Five

Getting off the Fence

By the time I finished graduate work at Nebraska, I had also been teaching for a couple of years and had been a graduate assistant coach working with the freshman football team. Then the chancellor of the university, Clifford Hardin, called me into his office and described a training program he had set up for people who wanted to go into college administration work. He offered me an opportunity. I thought it over and was mildly tempted, but I didn't feel I wanted to get entirely away from athletics. It had been too big a part of my life to quit cold turkey.

After that there was a period of four years when I tried to straddle the fence. I continued to teach undergraduate courses in educational psychology and was also teaching a graduate-level course or two. One of the graduate-level classes was in statistics, and my teaching it came as a shock. The statistics professor in the educational psychology department had resigned on very short notice, and I was told in the middle of August that I would be teaching the course starting in September.

I had taken only a couple of classes in that area, but it seemed as though the students really appreciated me as a teacher. I think the main reason was that I could get only about one page ahead of them in the textbook. I understood the problems they were going through because I had just gone through them the day before.

Teaching was challenging, and I also enjoyed coaching. I was unwilling to give up either. But after four years of this, I began to get pressure from people in the educational psychology department to make a commitment. I think they appreciated the teaching job I was doing, but they also wanted me to serve on graduate committees, be an academic advisor, and do all the other things that aren't particularly fun in the teaching profession. They also made it clear that success in education was dependent on doing research and publishing.

But at the same time I couldn't see myself getting out of athletics altogether, and I could see I wasn't going anywhere in coaching if I didn't get out, recruit, and become a full-time coach. Because of my teaching duties, I wasn't able to do much recruiting except when players came to the campus.

So it was in 1966 that I decided I wanted to be a full-time coach and went to talk to head coach Bob Devaney. Bob had turned the Nebraska program around with a 38-6 record since his arrival in Lincoln. Nebraska had only three winning seasons in the twenty-one years prior to Bob's arrival but had enjoyed four straight winning seasons under his coaching.

I explained to Bob what my aspirations were and asked for the large salary of ten thousand dollars. He agreed and said it would be fine with him if I became a full-time coach.

At that time there were no limits on the size of the coaching staff. I think we had seven or eight full-time coaches, three or four people, like myself, who were doing a little bit of graduate school and more or less a full-time coaching job, and then another three or four who were what we would now call graduate assistants, who did a little bit of coaching and a whole lot of studying.

Coaching looked like a pretty tough profession to me at that time because of the high attrition rate. The first coach I had with the Redskins, Mike Nixon, was fired after a couple of years. Bill McPeak followed him and lasted five or six years. Red Hickey was replaced after three or four years with the 49ers. And even back then the sports pages reported enough coaching changes to warn me that the average college coach lasted about five years, most pro coaches even less.

The only way I want to stay in this for any length of time, I thought, *is if I can be a head football coach where I can take control of my own destiny.* I remember setting a goal then of being a head coach by age thirty-five. I don't know why I picked that particular age. It seemed to me that most head coaches who were being hired then were really quite young. A lot of them were between thirty-two and thirty-five, so I guess thirty-five sounded like a good number. I was twenty-eight at that time.

I worked hard at being as good an assistant coach as I could be. I worked with the receivers—the split ends, flankers, and tight ends—and recruited in Kansas City, California, Arizona, and western Nebraska.

We had a fine season the first year I was in coaching as a full-time assistant. We won nine straight games before a Thanksgiving Day loss at Oklahoma on national television, when a short field goal won it 10-9 for the Sooners with forty-eight seconds remaining. We still won the Big Eight title, however, and went on to the Sugar Bowl, where Alabama took us apart 34-7 behind Kenny Stabler's 21 for 34, 201-yard passing performance.

The next two years were a struggle. In 1967 we won six games and lost to Kansas, Colorado, Missouri, and Oklahoma. We averaged twenty points a game less than in 1966 and failed to receive a bowl invitation for the first time in Bob's six years at the helm.

In 1968 the 6-4 record was repeated. There was no bowl invitation again. And worst of all, we were shut out 12-0 by Kansas State in the last home game, and then shut out again in the season finale at Oklahoma by the embarrassing score of 47-0. A humiliation on national television.

Many Nebraska fans now look at Bob Devaney's eleven years as head coach as "golden years," and they were. Yet things got rough after the second 6-4 season. Letters to the editor were nasty. There were suggestions that some assistant coaches should be replaced. There was even a petition circulated in Omaha to fire Bob. If my eyes had not been wide open concerning the vagaries of coaching previously, they were then. Here were people upset with a coach who had turned things around, who had moved Nebraska back into national prominence in football, and who hadn't had a losing season. How quickly things can change in athletics. But the 47-0 loss to Oklahoma to conclude a second 6-4 season proved to be a turning point in Nebraska football.

We had been having some difficulty moving the football. We felt our biggest problem was a lack of quality offensive linemen, so I mentioned to Bob that it would be a good idea if we went to California and recruited in the junior colleges, where we might be able to get immediate help. He agreed, so we went out to the West Coast and were able the first year to get three junior college players. One of them was an offensive lineman, one eventually became a linebacker, and one was a receiver. In 1969 we were able to get three more junior college offensive linemen and a receiver. All eventually played for us, and in 1970 and 1971—the two national championship years—our offensive line was mostly junior college players from California and Arizona.

We also had very fortunate high school recruiting years in 1967 and 1968 when we got some great offensive players—Guy Ingles, Johnny Rodgers, Jeff Kinney, Jerry Tagge, and Van Brownson. These people, along with defensive players such as Willie Harper, Rich Glover, Joe Blahak, Larry Jacobson, and John Dutton, became a great football team.

One of these great junior college offensive linemen told me on the phone when I was recruiting him that he was going to go to San Diego State. His name was Bob Newton, a huge (6'3", 250 pounds) rugged guy.

"Could I come over and see you one more time, Bob?" I asked.

"No, I've made up my mind," he replied.

At that time there was no limit to the number of times you could see a player, and I had already seen Bob a lot of times and had a good relationship with him. He sounded as though he really didn't want me to come because he knew I could influence him. But he had told me once earlier that he wanted to attend Nebraska.

So with that glimmer of hope I said, "Bob, you and I are pretty good friends. Can't we have just one more visit?" I knew if I got in the door one more time I would have a good chance to turn the big guy around. And I did.

Now when a player tells me he's going to another school, I say, "OK, good luck." But at that time I was really pushing hard. We needed offensive linemen badly. Bob came to Nebraska and eventually started at offensive tackle for us for two years, in 1969 and 1970, made some All-American teams in 1970, and played about eleven years of pro football.

Another player was Keith Wortman, an offensive lineman who was almost as big as Bob and was being recruited by the University of Southern California. At that time if you were being recruited by USC and lived in Southern California, it was a foregone conclusion where you were going to school. So I worked very hard on Keith, saw him time after time. USC coach John McKay lived not too far away, and I think maybe USC was taking Keith a little for granted. I kept bringing this up. "How many times has Coach McKay been over to see you?"

"Oh, I dunno," Keith responded.

I kept pointing out the great need we had for offensive linemen at Nebraska and the fact that Bob Devaney had been in his home and John McKay hadn't. Eventually Keith decided to come to Nebraska. He was not an overnight sensation, but he became a very good player for us at offensive guard and played seven or eight years of professional football.

We had a number of cases like Bob and Keith where I thought I was able to be successful in recruiting simply by outworking people—by *being* there a lot!

NCAA rules were changed in the mid-seventies, limiting the number of contacts to three visits at the school and three at the player's home. Under this rule I could not have been as successful because the schools closer to home—especially USC and UCLA—would easily have won out.

I worked very hard at recruiting because I felt it was probably the most important thing an assistant coach did, and I still feel that way. Recruiting is the life-blood of any college program, and it's probably the most difficult thing coaches do. The teams with the best players generally are the most successful. Good athletes make their coaches look good. It was true then and it is true now.

But recruiting changes weren't all that was needed in 1969. During an off-season meeting Bob said, "We need to change. I think it would be a good idea if we revamped our offense."

Until that time we had been using primarily an unbalanced line with a full-house backfield, somewhat similar to a wishbone setup. Oklahoma was doing well with the I-formation, so I tried to come up with some things on paper that looked reasonable out of the I. Bob checked these things and approved them. He said what he wanted to do and what he didn't want to do, and then we began to implement the new offense.

I don't think this change went over with great favor on the part of some of the other coaches who had been using the unbalanced line, full-house backfield since coaching with Bob at the University of Wyoming. But we did go ahead and implement the new offense. I was able to contribute to the offense by meeting daily with the quarterbacks on play selection and audibles, and I was also able to call some plays from the press box on game day.

In 1969, with the new offense and playing some sophomores, we started out winning two games and losing two, and things looked a little tough again. The new offense wasn't an overnight success. The reviews were mixed. However, we were playing well on defense.

Then we started to win and gradually became a very good football team. We avenged 1968's 47-0 loss to Oklahoma with a 44-14 win. We ended the regular season 8-2, tied for the conference championship, and went to the Sun Bowl for a 45-6 victory over Georgia. Things had turned around with a nine-game winning streak.

In 1970 and 1971, we had great football teams. In 1970 we were tied early in the season by USC out in Los Angeles, and then we won the rest of our games. So we were 10-0-1. We beat LSU in the Orange Bowl and were named national champions. We came from being rated third at the start of New Year's Day to number one when Texas and Ohio State were both upset.

The 1971 team really put things together. We went 13-0. We beat Oklahoma 35-31 in Norman in the last regular season game and then beat number-one-ranked Alabama 38-6 in the 1972 Orange Bowl. A perfect season. Another national championship. A great football team.

The Oklahoma-Nebraska game that year was called "The Game of the Century" by some, "The Game of the Decade" by others. It was at least "The Game of the Year" for me.

Going into the game we were undefeated and ranked first, Oklahoma undefeated and ranked second. We led the nation in most defensive statistics; Oklahoma led in many offensive stats. Greg Pruitt was their great All-American.

But Johnny Rodgers, who eventually became an All-American for us, got us going that day with a seventy-two-yard punt return for a touchdown early in the first quarter. Oklahoma came back to lead 17-14 at the half, but the seesaw continued and we went out front again 28-17 in the third quarter.

With just seven minutes left in the game, Oklahoma went ahead 31-28. But then our final victory march began, a drive that featured a great diving catch by Johnny on a third and eight situation and the running of Jeff Kinney, who finished with 174 yards for the day. We couldn't stop Oklahoma's wishbone offense, but we prevailed 35-31.

For the second time that season, the number one team played the number two in the nation when Nebraska met Alabama in the Orange Bowl, but this contest was nothing like the other battle of the top tandem. A seventy-seven-yard punt return by Johnny Rodgers was the most sparkling play in a stellar team performance that took us to a 28-0 half-time lead and a 34-6 final victory, particularly gratifying for Bob Devaney because it came over his old rival, Bear Bryant.

I remember sitting on the bus about 1:00 A.M. after the Orange Bowl game and on the way to the hotel, I thought, *This is supposed to be the epitome of what a person could experience in college football? Undefeated? National champions?* That squad was later voted to be the greatest football team of all time. Yet everybody just kind of sat there in a stupor.

I thought, *This isn't what it's supposed to be like!*

At the Ivanhoe Hotel about 2:00 A.M., I was sitting on the bed and Nancy said, "Come on. Everybody's celebrating. Let's *do* something." I just sat there.

"I'm going to go crazy," she said. "I'm going out and celebrate even if I just ride the elevator up and down all night!"

I sat there reflecting, *It really isn't so much achieving the end result—the national championship and the trophies, which are all fine. But the important thing about athletics really is the process. It's the path you follow in attempting to win the championship that's important. The relationships that are formed. The effort given. The experiences you have. And when it's over, it's all over!* Everything else, at least for me, was kind of an anti-climax.

Of course, one might say, "Well, you felt that way because you weren't the head coach at the time." I really don't believe that. I think I experienced things every bit as strongly emotionally as an assistant in the press box as I do now on the sidelines as head coach. The wins and the losses, the disappointments and high moments—I felt them very much then as I do now.

The only thing different in being head coach is you're more out front. You're more obvious to other people. As a result, you're more of a lightning rod. You seem to get more praise when you win and more blame when you lose. But still I think the feelings—the elation and the disappointment—are felt just as keenly when you're an assistant coach or a player.

And what I was feeling that night on the bus and in the hotel has stayed with me ever since as a head coach. The joy is in the striving, more than in arriving. I love the *process*—the preparation, the effort, the strategy, the players, the games. The results are somewhat anti-climactic.

Chapter Six

Following a Legend

Memories of 6-4 seasons in 1967 and 1968, the fatigue of a hard-fought 10-7 road victory over Kansas State, and the prospect of a long bus ride back from Manhattan to Lincoln may have had Bob Devaney pretty drained.

Sitting there in the bus with him as we bumped and swayed our way north, Bob said to me, "I don't want to go much longer. Maybe another year or so. I'd like you to take over as head coach."

I was really surprised. Thinking back to that late autumn Saturday in 1969, I would say Bob had hit a low point. We had just played a very demanding game and come off two seasons that had taken a lot out of him. While 6-4 seasons were looked upon with favor at a lot of places, in Nebraska, after a series of 10-1 seasons, two 6-4 seasons without championships and bowl games were hard for people to take.

Then came the 1970 and 1971 seasons, and Bob was not quite as ready to retire. He had indicated that he would probably retire after the 1971 season, but then decided to stay on one more year in an attempt to win three consecutive national championships.

I really had not aspired to be the head coach at Nebraska. I wanted to go somewhere else where I could develop my own staff and my own ideas. I thought following Bob would be a very difficult task because he had turned the program around and was very popular. I thought anyone who followed him would be in for a hard time.

I was interviewed at the University of South Dakota for the head football job in 1968. Joe Salem was the other finalist for the job. Joe was originally from South Dakota and had been a player and assistant coach at Minnesota. Joe was hired instead of me and eventually went on to coach at Northern Arizona and at the University of Minnesota.

I was offered a job at Augustana College in South Dakota a year or so later. I seriously considered that because it was a fairly small college where teaching was to be part of the job. I was really tempted to take the job because I would have enjoyed the teaching aspect of it. But I also knew that if I went into Division II football, it was quite possible I would be locked into that level and would never reach the major colleges. I really wasn't all that enamored with major college football, and yet I thought I might always wonder if I could have made it in Division I. Nancy and I went up to Augustana, looked around, and really thought it through carefully. We were tempted to go but finally turned the job down.

At the conclusion of the 1969 season, I applied at Texas Tech University. I went to Lubbock for an interview immediately following our victory over Georgia in the Sun Bowl (Nancy was in Lincoln in the hospital, having just given birth to our youngest child, Suzi). I was one of two people they were considering for the job. I was supposedly at the top of a list of assistant coaches. Jim Carlin was the top candidate on a list of head coaches. They finally offered the job to Jim, who at that time was head coach at West Virginia.

I was excited about Texas Tech because I thought it had a lot of possibilities, was a good school, and would have given me a chance to start on my own. And while I was doing this applying, Bob kept talking to me about staying at Nebraska, saying he would like to see me stay on another year or two and that he was definitely planning to step aside at some point.

After the 1971 season, Bob got the coaches together in the hotel down at the Orange Bowl. We had just beaten Alabama for the national championship. He announced he was going to coach for one more year and I was going to be his successor. I was given the title of Assistant Head Coach.

I had mixed feelings. I was pleased I was going to get the chance to be a head coach, and I realized there were an awful lot of assistant coaches who wanted to be head coaches who never got the opportunity. I didn't feel I could very well turn it down, because I might never get another opportunity somewhere else. And yet at the same time, if I were to be a head coach, I really didn't want to follow Bob Devaney. But I guess I wanted to be a head coach more than I wanted to coach somewhere Bob hadn't been, so I stayed at Nebraska. Nebraska was attractive because of the tradition, the facilities, the people, and the fact that it was my home. The difficult part would be Bob's shadow.

Bob had a good touch with people—a good sense of when to push the team, when to drive them, when to get angry with them, when to ease off, and when to be friendly. He had a very easy way about him and a good sense of humor. He was also an excellent public speaker.

Another thing he did so well, I thought, was give someone a job to do and then not interfere too much. When he gave me the job as academic counselor or coach of receivers or quarterbacks, naturally he wanted to know what was going on, but he didn't try to do the job for me after giving it to me.

We never had offensive or defensive coordinators under Bob. I guess I had been as close to being the offensive coordinator as you could be without having a title, and Monte Kiffin did most of the things a defensive coordinator normally does during Bob's last few years as head coach. Bob was very good at using his people. And I think he had a good deal of loyalty from his staff as a result of the way he operated.

Bob had a temper, and at times he could be a fairly hard driving, demanding coach. One thing that was sure to set him off was a quarterback sack. I remember particularly a practice one spring when we just couldn't keep the defensive line off our quarterbacks, and Bob really got angry. At one point I couldn't find our offensive backfield coach, Mike Corgan. I looked all around for him and finally located him sitting high up in the end-zone stands, smoking his pipe. He'd just had enough of the fireworks.

But Bob never stayed mad for very long and had a great sense of timing, of when to back off and have a little fun in practice. He was good at getting the most out of his players. His attempts to joke around with the players—to exist at their level off the field some, to be a little more human—have been important to me because I have a tendency to concentrate so hard on football and be such a perfectionist that this element of humanness can be lost.

The last year Bob was the coach, 1972, was a unique situation in that it is very seldom a coach will set things up where everyone has a year to get used to the heir apparent. Usually coaches either get fired or resign on rather short notice, so a gradual transition is impossible. In this case Bob was in a strong enough position to name his successor, and it went smoothly. All the assistant coaches had a year to sit back, think about the situation, and look at me as a potential head coach. The players had the same opportunity. Everything was fairly cut and dried.

Of course, it was good of the university administration to go along with Bob's recommendation. I think many of them had some concern because here I was, thirty-four years old and someone relatively unknown and unproved, taking over a very successful program and following a very successful man. Of course, Bob was the athletic director as well, which didn't hurt.

The season following Bob's announcement was a hard one for me because I saw I was going to accept responsibility for the whole program. Recruiting became especially important to me. It had been important before but was even more urgent now. Everything in the program was becoming more vital to me.

The 1972 season made it a little easier to succeed Bob in that we didn't go undefeated. We won 9, lost 2, and tied 1. We lost 17-14 to Oklahoma the last game in Lincoln but still won the conference championship technically because Oklahoma had to forfeit three games. We went to the Orange Bowl, where we beat Notre Dame 40-6. We had some exciting players including Johnny Rodgers, who was in his senior year. Because of our success we got a lot of national attention, but it was not as difficult for me as having to take over after another national championship would have been.

Still, in his last three years, Bob Devaney had lost only two games, had two ties, and won two national championships. So there was a fairly heavy load of expectation on me.

Chapter Seven

Silencing the Critics (a Little)

"When I first took over as head coach," I told those gathered at the 1973 Big Eight Kickoff Luncheon in Kansas City, my first as head coach, "I was very nervous. We had thirteen starters missing and we'd had ten players drafted by the pros. On top of that, I was replacing the nation's winningest coach.

"But I have read a lot of magazine and newspaper articles recently indicating that all Nebraska has to do to win the Big Eight is to show up. And that unless the coach messes up, Nebraska will be national champion.

"So I'm real relaxed about the coming season."

My debut as a head coach a few weeks later made national television. UCLA had beaten us the year before 17-14 in Los Angeles and was favored to beat us again. But our team played an emotional game, worked very hard, and won 40-13. We were tremendously physical, really pushing around a very good UCLA team (they ended the season 9-2). It was an amazing turnaround from 1972.

I was interested in how I would react as a head coach. How would it feel on the sideline as opposed to being in the press box? Would the

added responsibility cause me to think or respond any differently from
the way I had as an assistant coach? I found I did not. I was no more
nervous, uptight, or upset than I had been as an assistant. I discovered I responded in just about the same way.

The opening victory, which vaulted us to number two in the nation,
was followed by wins over North Carolina State, Wisconsin, and Minnesota.

In the Wisconsin game, the score was tied 7-7 after three quarters,
and then the game really got wild. Midway through the final period,
Wisconsin kicked a twenty-nine-yard field goal to move ahead 10-7.
But we came back on an eighty-yard march in just six plays, with
David Humm connecting on a little delay pass over the middle to
Frosty Anderson, who outran the man-to-man coverage for twenty-
three yards and the touchdown. Now it was 14-10 Nebraska, with five
and one-half minutes to play.

Our joy turned to sorrow—no, maybe it was shock!—when Wisconsin returned our kickoff ninety-six yards to go back on top 16-14.

We learned a lot about what our team was made of, though, when
we got up from the mat and marched eighty-three yards in seven
plays. Humm completed three passes, Ritch Bahe gained forty yards
on an inside reverse, and Tony Davis went over from fourteen yards
out for the winning touchdown.

It was the first "character win"—a time to see what a team is made
of—in my head coaching career. It was quite satisfying. And David
Humm was simply brilliant in a 25 for 36, 297-yard passing day—a
school record.

My first defeat as a head coach was at Missouri against the highly
ranked Tigers, and I suppose it started the tradition I have become
most famous (or infamous) for: going for two.

The teams were deadlocked 6-6 after three quarters of play despite
our piling up nearly two hundred yards in passing by Humm and holding Missouri to minus yardage passing. Then it happened. The Tigers—before their home crowd—turned our fumbled punt return into
a quick score and 13-6 lead late in the game.

But just as in the Wisconsin game, our players showed they were
resilient. With only two minutes remaining we began a dramatic drive.
Humm to Bahe for thirty-one yards. Humm to Larry Muzhinskie for

twenty yards. Humm to Bahe for the touchdown. Score 13-12 and one minute left. There was no choice but to go for the win.

And there was really not much question but that we should try a pass play with Humm's hot hand (he was 20 of 30 for 290 yards for the day). But Frosty Anderson had separated his shoulder early in the game, and his replacement, Dave Shamblin, was so out of gas by this point that he couldn't get to the ball, so we tasted defeat for the first time that season and in my head coaching career.

It was a weird game. Missouri won 13-12, but we had 444 yards of total offense and Missouri had about 180. We did a poor job on kickoff coverage, had a field goal blocked, and had a couple of injuries in the game. It was just a whole series of things that reversed on us. Normally with the statistics we had and the way we played, we would have won by two or three touchdowns. It was a very disappointing loss, and yet I found, as with winning, that I really didn't feel a whole lot different about losing as a head coach than I did as an assistant.

But apparently the game took a lot out of the team. The next week only a blocked extra point allowed us to beat Kansas 10-9, and then we tied Oklahoma State 17-17 when a fourth down run failed to score from OSU's half-yard line late in the game. I took a little heat for ignoring the field goal and going for the touchdown. It was my first truly controversial decision.

We bounced back with a 28-16 win over Colorado, gained momentum with a 31-7 victory over Iowa State, and then accumulated over six hundred yards against Kansas State in a 50-21 win in which Tony Davis and Johnny O'Leary each gained more than one hundred yards rushing for us.

Then came the low point of my first season as head coach: a 27-0 loss to Oklahoma at Norman. Everybody had something bad to say about the effort. Headlines read: "Huskers Discover Futility" and "NU Tilts." Subtitles pointed out other subtleties: "First Time in 58 Games Huskers Fail to Score." "Penetrate Sooner Territory Only Once." Words like "whipped" and "routed" punctuated most accounts of the game.

But while our 4-2-1 record in the conference and the season-ending shutout made this an unhappy season for some of our fans, the Cotton Bowl committee saw more: an 8-2-1 record overall and a loyal following that would support us on New Year's Day in Dallas.

Losing to Oklahoma 27-0 not only made the fans unhappy, but it also made the players unhappy. And while the coaching staff decided we were going to work very hard to try to play well against Texas in the Cotton Bowl, one of our captains decided that a bowl game was a reward for a good season and that you ought to have a good time and not put forth much effort. I didn't really resent his feeling, but he called a team meeting with none of the coaches present and expressed these views, which I felt were contrary to the purpose of football and the role of a captain. So the captain and I had a falling out, and he was dismissed from the team for a period of time.

Eventually he apologized to the coaches and the team, was reinstated, and played well in the game. It was part of the process of adjustment from one coach to another, from one system to another. It was one thing that just had to be weathered. Time took care of a lot of these things.

More than twenty thousand loyal Nebraskans migrated to Dallas for the Cotton Bowl, and our defense rewarded them with a 19-3 win over a highly favored Texas team led by Roosevelt Leaks. Ogallala, Nebraska, walk-on Steve Runty, who had quarterbacked our opening win against UCLA but hadn't played a lot since, was the spark in our breaking the game open after a 3-3 deadlock at the half.

In that first season I was criticized for:
- being too conservative in our 10-9 win over Kansas,
- being too aggressive in going for two points in our 13-12 loss to Missouri,
- gambling too much in going for the touchdown rather than the field goal in the 17-17 tie against Oklahoma State, and
- being too nice.

It's terribly hard to please everybody in this profession.

It was ironic. That first year we ended up with a 9-2-1 record, which was exactly the same record Bob Devaney had in 1972, his last year as the head coach. But, in the two prior years, 1970 and 1971, Bob had been undefeated and had won national championships; so the 9-2-1 record was not really met with great enthusiasm. And of course we had also graduated players such as Johnny Rodgers and some other great athletes that made the 1972 team a little more spectacular than our 1973 group. But the Cotton Bowl win in 1973 did silence the critics to some degree and salvage, I think, a fairly good season.

Immediately after our Cotton Bowl victory, Texas head coach Darryl Royal, a seventeen-year veteran of that position, came to our locker room to congratulate the team and me. That impressed me— it's unusual for coaches to do that—and it led me to being closer to Darryl for a time than most other opposing coaches.

Darryl and I walked out of the locker room together to talk, and before parting he said in his southern drawl, "What a coach needs to do after losing a bowl game is just slide away for a few days and let things simmer." And he did just that.

It's crossed my mind to do this a couple of times since.

Chapter Eight

Getting the Monkey off Our Back...and on It Again

O ne of the highest points of my coaching career was the Oklahoma game of 1978. We had lost seven straight years to Oklahoma, and there had been quite a bit of unrest among the Nebraska fans. That year we played a great Oklahoma team, possibly as talented as any Oklahoma team that we had faced, and we were able to beat them with a good but not a great team, 17-14, in Lincoln. That got a little bit of the monkey off our backs. But that game was followed within a week by one of the lowest points of my coaching career.

We had entered the Oklahoma game with a 8-1 record, having won eight straight since a 20-3 opening loss to number-one-ranked Alabama on national television.

The eight straight wins did not start easily—36-26 over California, with twenty-two points coming in the fourth quarter. But we were rolling up a lot of yards and points all season, with I-backs I.M. Hipp and Rick Berns getting most of the attention.

We gained 599 yards in a 56-10 win over Hawaii, then beat Indiana 69-17, Iowa State 23-0, Kansas State 48-14, Colorado 52-14, Oklahoma State 22-14, and finally Kansas 63-21 with a Big Eight-record 799 yards.

The scores do not reflect the closeness of a couple of the games. Colorado held a 14-3 lead at one point. And the win against Oklahoma State was preserved only by a game-saving tackle by defensive end Derrie Nelson on one play and an errant pass to a wide-open OSU receiver on another. OSU actually outgained us by a few yards for the day.

So these scares and the millstone of never having beaten Oklahoma had me concerned as we returned to Lincoln to prepare for the Sooners. It had been several years since Nebraska had beaten Oklahoma 35-31 in the so-called "Game of the Century."

Beating Oklahoma became somewhat of an obsession to fans in Nebraska. It became the biggest game of the year for us, and there was all kinds of media attention. Usually the game meant the conference championship or at least a share of it. We had some close calls over the years, and yet we weren't able to beat them. And of course the perception developed that I was unable to beat Oklahoma. "Osborne can't win the big one," folks said.

I felt it was not just a case of *our* not beating Oklahoma. *Nobody* was beating Oklahoma!

During that period Barry Switzer had won well over 90 percent of his games and had great personnel, great defenses. Most of the games they had lost were early in the year when they weren't as well organized. They were just a very difficult team to beat by the end of the season in a big football game, which was always the case when we played them.

Nebraska fans weren't the only folks who were making victory over Oklahoma an obsession. My friend Darryl Royal also had a serious case of the "Oklahoma obsession." Darryl used to call me two or three times a year, and our conversations would usually turn to Oklahoma. Neither of us was having much luck with them at the time.

Even my daughter Ann got into the act. After one of the losses, Nancy gathered the kids in the kitchen and asked, "What are we going to say to Dad when he gets home? You know he'll feel bad, so let's figure out things that will make him feel better."

Signals thus checked, they awaited my arrival. When I reached the house and walked through the door, everybody recited their rehearsed lines. And then Ann, who still hates to lose, announced, "I'm going to move to Oklahoma if we lose to them again!"

I never felt like panicking or got as uptight about it as some people thought I did. We thought that if we recruited hard and prepared well, we could put together a better football team. We believed football would be cyclical and eventually we would be successful.

But I had to admit, after the sixth straight loss, including five since I had become head coach, that I was beginning to wonder if I would survive long enough as a coach to beat Oklahoma. I began to realize this was something the fans were going to expect to happen or, no matter how good the record was overall, there would be a lot of pressure to get a different coach. Lots of fans did not feel this way, but I think there were many in Nebraska who did, and they were vocal enough that they made things uncomfortable.

It's occurred to me often that many problems in athletics—perhaps *most* problems—result from people having an inappropriate understanding of athletics. The problem with some fans, for example, is that they get their sense of worth, or lack of it, from the athletic team they support. They often have inadequate feelings about themselves, so if the team wins, the fans win. If the team loses, the fans lose and they begin to feel worse about themselves.

It was my spiritual life during this period that gave me balance. If the most important thing had been the won-lost record, then I'd have hung my hat on something that's very tenuous, because the won-lost record is going to fluctuate. You cannot always be as successful as other people want you to be. Having a spiritual dimension, a certain spiritual depth, a reliance on God's grace, was very important during those years, and still is. When you begin to realize that the most important thing is not whether you win or lose football games, but rather your relationship to Him, then things acquire a certain perspective that diminishes the ups and downs—the emotionalism that often accompanies coaching and is very destructive.

Oklahoma arrived in Lincoln in 1978 with a great back in Billy Sims who scored the game's first points on a forty-four-yard run mid-way

through the first quarter. We tied the game on a five-yard run by Rick
Berns early in the second quarter and then went ahead early in the
second half when I. M. Hipp scored on a run from eight yards out.
But Sims brought the Sooners right back with a thirty-yard run two
minutes later, tying the score at 14-14.

Early in the fourth quarter, Billy Todd hit a twenty-four-yard field
goal to put us in front 17-14, and on the ensuing kick-off John Ruud
popped Oklahoma return man Kelly Phillips with a tremendous tackle
that jarred the ball loose. We recovered deep in Oklahoma territory
and it appeared we had the game under control. Only there was a
problem—the officials didn't see the play our way and didn't give us
the ball.

They ruled no fumble. There was a lot of complaining by our fans. I
called the team together and told them they were going to have to play
over the breaks.

The drama increased as Oklahoma drove closer toward our goal line
late in the game. But Sims coughed up the ball at our three yard line
with just 3:27 to play, and this time we kept the ball. It was Oklahoma's ninth fumble of the day, six of which we recovered (seven if you
asked our fans).

It was a great defensive effort and snapped the so-called jinx. We
won at least a share of the conference championship and received an
"unofficial" invitation to the Orange Bowl. We did not know whom we
would play there.

But the ecstasy didn't last long.

We had very little left emotionally after the Oklahoma game, and we
were really sore and beaten up physically. And so the next week
against Missouri we came up just short, losing 35-31 despite a school
record-breaking 255 yards rushing by Rick Berns. Missouri had
equally outstanding play from James Wilder and Kellen Winslow and
stopped us on a fourth down play deep in their territory as time ran
out.

In the crowded, steamy, and decidedly downcast locker room after
the game, a couple of members of the Orange Bowl committee advised me we would get a call in a few minutes to receive our official
invitation to the Orange Bowl and learn who our opponent would be.

The call came in and we were extended the official invitation to the

Orange Bowl. Then the lightning bolt: "And your opponent will be Oklahoma."

"What?" we all said. "We just beat them a week ago!" Amidst all the speculation regarding our opponent, there'd been no hint that Oklahoma was an option.

But it was true.

What a blow! Losing to Missouri and learning we would have to play Oklahoma twice within a period of seven weeks, particularly after finally having beaten them for the first time in seven years, put me as low as I'd ever been in coaching. It took quite a bit of the glow off our Oklahoma win and what had been a great season.

There were two times in those first six years when I wanted to chuck it all. The first was in 1976 when we let Oklahoma off the hook in the final moments of the game with two long passing plays, one a flea-flicker, and lost 20-17. That had been my fourth straight loss to Oklahoma.

This was the second time.

So conference co-champions squared off in the Orange Bowl. And instead of playing Penn State for the national championship, we were faced with merely confirming our conference championship. I was frustrated at having to play Oklahoma again. We realized we would be at quite a psychological disadvantage in the game because Oklahoma would be out to avenge the only loss it had that year.

At the Orange Bowl we jumped off to a 7-0 lead, but this was one of the really great, really explosive Sooner teams, and they stormed back and built a 31-10 lead entering the fourth quarter.

Oklahoma had a more talented team than we did, and although we finally lost the game by a touchdown, we came back on them and made them sweat it out at the end.

I thought we played about as well as we could under the circumstances. Oklahoma had Sims, a great back, Thomas Lott at quarterback, and a number of other great athletes. I thought our team played very hard and showed a lot of character. So even though we lost the game, I felt as though we had done our best, that we were successful in the Orange Bowl game, and therefore I did not really take the loss so hard. I resented the circumstances that had put us there, but I was still proud of the way we responded to that situation.

Some thought it was kind of a cruel season, and the monkey that we had gotten off our backs in November had climbed back on in January. I just noted that as low points are followed by highs, so high points are followed by lows, which is why coaches need to measure their success and their worth by some other standard than winning percentages and fan reactions.

Chapter Nine

Staying Put

In the two dozen years I've been at the University of Nebraska, the only time I seriously contemplated leaving was after the 1978 season. My restlessness may have been prompted by the up-and-down nature of that campaign, culminating with the disappointment of playing Oklahoma a second time that season in the Orange Bowl.

All the coaches and our families were suffering a little from the fact that we'd had good seasons in the six years I had been head coach, never winning fewer than nine games and going to a bowl game every year, and yet the feeling persisted in many people that we really hadn't been very successful because we had beaten Oklahoma only once and had only a couple of ties for the Big Eight championship to show for our efforts. Certainly our record had not been viewed with great enthusiasm by the fans, and I think all of us were tempted to go somewhere where winning eight or nine games in a year would be appreciated to a greater degree.

Whatever the reason, I did explore another coaching position in December of 1978. When Bill Mallory, the University of Colorado football coach, left at the end of that season, I talked on the phone about the job with my friend Dean Brittenham, who was the head track coach there at the time. Dean was quite positive about the overall athletic program at Colorado and must have relayed some of our conversation to Eddie Crowder, who was then their athletic director. Eddie called me the next day and expressed some interest, and I told him I would think it over, but that I wouldn't come out to look at the campus unless I was reasonably sure I was going to make the move. I spent the next day or two talking to Nancy and our assistant coaches, and they all seemed to be supportive of taking a good look at Colorado.

Colorado had some excellent athletes in the late sixties and early and middle seventies. For much of that period, they had more players in professional football than either Nebraska or Oklahoma. Even though both Nebraska and Oklahoma had generally beaten Colorado during that period, it seemed Colorado was a place where coaches could do a good recruiting job. And, of course, I do love to fish for trout, and the trout streams aren't too far away from Boulder, where the university is located.

I finally told Eddie Crowder that I would like to come out and take a look, that I was serious about the job. If everything checked out, I would definitely make the move. Nancy and I flew to Boulder and met with Eddie and a number of key boosters. I also talked to my friend Dan Stavely, who had been an assistant coach at Colorado for a number of years. I tried to get as good a feel for the facilities and the overall situation as you could get in one day's visit.

When we got back on the plane to Lincoln, I wasn't quite as positive as I had been that this was the move we needed to make. As we flew home, I reflected on the fact that one of the things at Nebraska that I had previously viewed as negative was the way we lived in such a goldfish bowl almost year round because of the great interest in Nebraska football. It seemed as though we never got away from close scrutiny concerning the program. I had thought that making a move to Colorado would alleviate some of this constant pressure, and after visiting there, I was sure the pressure would be less.

However, I could also see that this was true because there wasn't the same degree of unity concerning University of Colorado football as there was around University of Nebraska football. In Nebraska, many of the people have lived in the state most of their lives, and they have only one real loyalty as far as major college football is concerned, and that is the University of Nebraska. Also, there are no pro teams to compete for attention. In Colorado, the population is somewhat transitory, so there is no real deep-seated feeling on the part of most people about University of Colorado football. The major football interest is the Denver Broncos, and, of course, there is Colorado State University and the Air Force Academy too.

The facilities at Colorado were good, but not as good as those we had at Nebraska. The salary and fringe benefits Eddie Crowder had talked about would have exceeded the money I was making at Nebraska, and there were many other positive features about the Colorado program.

But as I thought the matter through, I realized the greatest obstacle to the move was the Nebraska players. I really didn't want to tell the young men we had recruited to Nebraska that we were leaving. I had told so many of them that I planned to be at Nebraska for a long time. So I finally decided the best place for me was still the University of Nebraska.

The whole exercise proved to have some unexpected results. After looking at Colorado, I had renewed appreciation for the positive features we have at the University of Nebraska. And when we appeared to be on our way to Colorado, the Nebraska fans showed a little greater appreciation for the accomplishments of our coaching staff and expressed the desire to see us stay. It was a turning point.

In the years since 1978, there have been a few other opportunities to leave Nebraska. One of the most unusual occurred when an alumnus from a southern school called and indicated he had been designated to speak for that institution and that he would guarantee, through a personal services contract, that I would double my income if I went to that school. I thought this was rather unusual in that the man had never met me, I had not been there for an interview, and I hadn't expressed any interest in the job. The school was an excellent school and they had a fine football program, but after thinking it over for only a few minutes, I told him I was really not interested because I had decided to say at Nebraska and I really didn't like the idea of working primarily for one person. The gentleman who had called was a very wealthy oil man, and I could imagine that his patience might wear thin in a hurry if his money didn't produce the results he wanted.

The only professional job I've been offered that was of some interest to me was with the Seattle Seahawks. I knew they had strong and stable ownership, I knew several of the players on the Seahawks, and the city of Seattle appeared to be one of the better NFL cities in which to live. Again, of course, there was that matter of fishing nearby. I declined their offer because my main interest is in working with college athletes in the more formative stages of their development. I also like the idea of being affiliated with a university and the academic community.

I suppose my strong roots as a Nebraskan and my liking for the state, the people, and the players, have really been overriding factors in all of these decisions. They have certainly been more important than financial considerations, and I suspect I will end my coaching career at Nebraska. Right now that's what I want. In athletics, however, you learn to never say "never." Things can change so quickly.

Chapter Ten

The Quarterbacks

Before the 1979 Cotton Bowl game in Dallas, eight or nine little kids cornered one of our players for autographs when I was leaving the hotel for the stadium. When they saw me, someone yelled, "There he is!" and the kids rushed toward me thrusting pens and paper into my stomach.

About the same time, though, our leading rusher, Isaiah Hipp, was strolling out of the hotel elevator. I had just written "Tom" on a piece of paper for a boy when another yelled, "There he is!" The kid pulled the pen and paper out of my hand, leaving the autograph half done, and rushed toward Isaiah.

There's a lesson in this. The game is for the *players*, not the coaches.

My coaching philosophy began to be shaped when I was a player in high school, college, and professional athletics. I can remember how I felt when I was unjustly criticized, when a coach didn't really understand why some things happened. I felt then and now that it is really important for players to sense that the coach is trying to understand, trying to see things from their viewpoint and not simply using them as pawns in a game. I know many times I resented that a coach seemed to look at a player as an object, someone only to accomplish his ends and his purposes.

So I guess I've carried some of that with me into coaching and have tried as best I can to be sympathetic, to look at things through the eyes of the players and not give them the feeling that they're objects, but rather people who are important. Whether a person is on the fourth team or the first, he has equal value as a human being. The fourth teamer doesn't have the same value to the football team as a first stringer, but as a human being—as a person—he does have the same value, and he ought to sense that by the access, time, and encouragement I give to him.

My greatest satisfaction in coaching has come in the relationship with players. I admire them greatly. I admire their courage, dedication, and openness to life. Usually people who play football are willing to take risks, and usually people who are willing to take risks are the most alive kind of people.

Over the years, the players I have been closest to are the quarterbacks, because I work with them personally every day.

The first quarterback I had much to do with was stocky Jerry Tagge from Green Bay, Wisconsin. He had the appearance of a hearty linebacker. Jerry was actually the third quarterback on the freshman team. He was a little heavy and couldn't move well. He sprained his ankle right away and had even less mobility. I remember some talk during the winter of making him a center. But he wanted to stay at quarterback and came out in the spring and did better.

In his sophomore year, Jerry and Van Brownson alternated at quarterback. Each of them started from time to time. Jerry was a little stronger and more durable player, while Van was quicker. Jerry kept getting better each year, and Van leveled off due, at least in part, to injuries. So by their junior years, Jerry played most of the time. In his senior year, Jerry played practically all the time.

Jerry ended up an All-American. He was a good thrower with a strong arm, he ran 4.9 in the forty-yard dash, and he operated the option better than you would think a 4.9 guy could do it.

He was drafted in 1972 in the first round by the Green Bay Packers, his home-town team. That may have turned out to be more of a curse than a blessing because so much was expected of him back in his home community. He was to be the answer to everybody's prayers for

My dad with Jack (left) and me in July 1942.

In uniform as a third-baseman at age 15.

Scoring two points on the fast break for Hastings College.

The high school coach who said I wasn't tough enough motivated me to scrap more and become a better player. I'm the guy on the floor.

Discus throwing was
my field event.

In track, I ran but hated the 440.

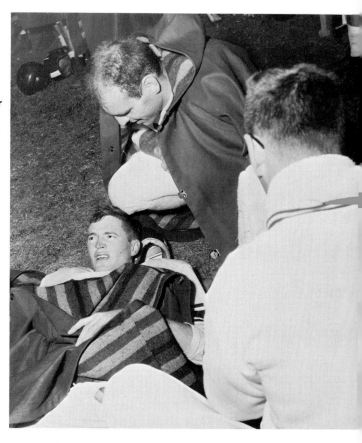

I was utterly exhausted after our upset win over Kearney State in 1958.

Carrying the ball (number 31) for Hastings College.

My brother, Jack (number 30), was a freshman at Hastings College in 1959. I was a senior.

This shot was taken at a practice during my professional football days.

With Mom and Dad the day I
received my master's degree,
June 8, 1963.

Mike was in my arms and a
Ph.D. was in my pocket on this
day in August 1965.

Two of my biggest fans in 1969, Mike (age 4½) and Ann (age 2).

With daughter Suzi on the day in 1972 when I was publicly named Cornhusker head coach.

My first coaching staff in 1973. Front row (from left): Warren Powers, Jim Anderson, Mike Corgan, Guy Ingles, Jerry Moore, and John Melton. Standing in the back row (from left): Cletus Fischer, Rick Duval, Monte Kiffin, me, Bill Myles, Jim Ross, and George Darlington. Photo by University of Nebraska Photographic Productions.

Good assistant coaches are the backbone of any program. I've been fortunate to have many such men including Lance Van Zandt (middle) and Charlie McBride (right). Photo by University of Nebraska Photographic Productions.

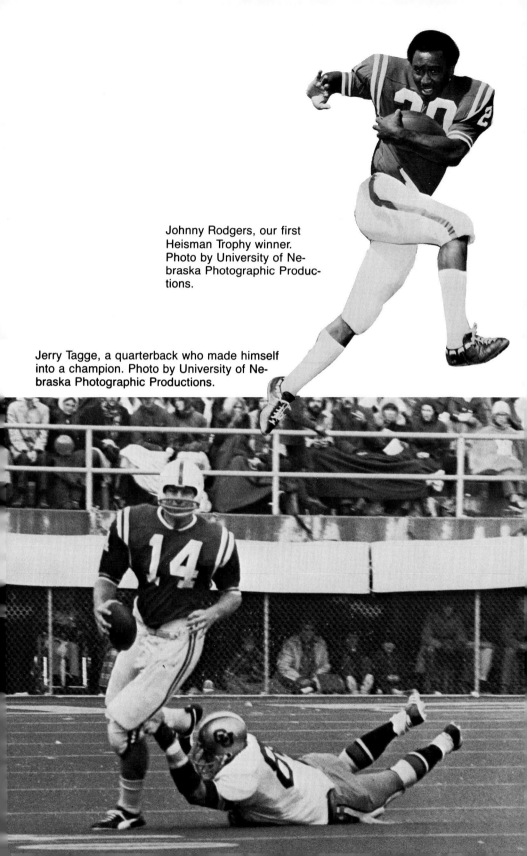

Johnny Rodgers, our first Heisman Trophy winner. Photo by University of Nebraska Photographic Productions.

Jerry Tagge, a quarterback who made himself into a champion. Photo by University of Nebraska Photographic Productions.

One of the best college linemen in recent years was Dean Steinkuhler (number 71). Photo by University of Nebraska Photographic Productions.

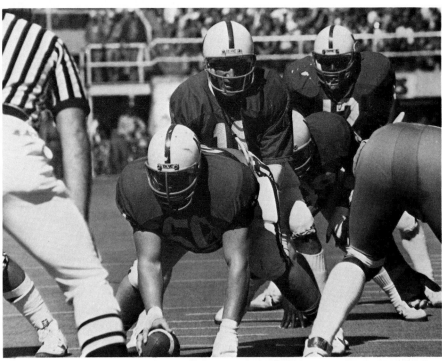

Dave Rimington (number 50) was not only a top lineman but also one of the strongest Cornhuskers ever. Photo by University of Nebraska Photographic Productions.

Two of the finest athletes I've had the privilege to coach, Mike Rozier (left) and Turner Gill. Photo by the Lincoln *Journal-Star.*

Whether throwing or running, Turner Gill was the ideal quarterback for the Nebraska offense. Photos by University of Nebraska Photographic Productions.

Mike Rozier holds nearly every Nebraska rushing record and is one of the finest runners I've ever seen. Photos by University of Nebraska Photographic Productions.

Irving Fryar (number 27) was another great all-around athlete. His speed and versatility made him the number 1 pick in the NFL draft. Photo above by the Lincoln *Journal-Star*. Photo at right by University of Nebraska Photographic Productions.

A large part of coaching is teaching, and that continues even on the sidelines during a game. Photo by University of Nebraska Photographic Productions.

A time-out strategy discussion with my assistants in the press box. Turner Gill (helmet in hand) and Irving Fryar (number 27) wait for my decision on the next play call. Photo by University of Nebraska Photographic Productions.

With Mike at a practice prior to our ill-fated Orange Bowl game against the University of Miami. Photo by the Lincoln *Journal-Star.*

The Osborne family in December 1984. Behind Nancy and me are (left to right) Suzi, Mike, and Ann. Photo by Ted Kirk.

the Packers. There's always a lot of pressure on quarterbacks, but it was more than normal in his case. He just wasn't able to succeed there. Maybe he wasn't ready to be thrust into that situation. Then he bounced around in pro football and eventually had some success in Canadian football before an injury ended his career.

But for us he was a steady performer, a good player on some great teams, the 1970 and 1971 national championship squads. He still holds Nebraska's total offense records—passing and running yardage, in Jerry's case—for a single game (319 yards), season (2,333 yards), and career (5,283 yards). Not bad for a lead-footed third-stringer whom we wanted to make into a center.

We asked David Humm to red-shirt during the 1971 season because we had both Tagge and Brownson going into their senior years. We worked David a lot in practice with the first and second offensive units and prepared him to play the next year.

David was a pure dropback thrower—the archetypical passer, although left-handed. He had been heavily recruited by nearly every major school and provided the most intense recruiting battle with which I've ever been associated. At the time of David's recruitment, rules allowed us to take a player out to eat, and we could see him an unlimited number of times. And David didn't sign until April or early May, so it was not only an intense recruiting battle but also a long one.

I don't know whether it was because David was such a great player, because he lived in Las Vegas, or both, but more coaches put in more time and spent more money recruiting David than any player I've known about before or since. Bear Bryant was out there several times and even took Joe Namath with him. I can remember meeting heavyweight champion Joe Frazier with David at Caesar's Palace. I know I was with him at Circus Circus until 2:00 A.M. on a school night on another occasion. Bob Devaney was out there several times, and John Melton, our assistant who did most of the recruiting involving David, was in Las Vegas weekly for four or five months.

An evening out would often cost one hundred dollars, so it was a welcome relief when the NCAA declared a few years later that you could no longer take a recruit or his family out for dinner or entertainment. Limiting the number of recruiting contacts to three at the prospect's school and three at his home is also a good rule, even though I resisted it at the time it was passed. The recruiting calendar—limiting personal recruiting visits to December, January, and February in football—has also been a step in the right direction. It cuts down recruiting time and expense and takes some of the pressure off recruits.

At any rate, David signed with Nebraska and had a great college career, leading the Big Eight in passing for three years. His main asset was throwing accuracy and a very quick release. He was bright and could run well enough to get by, but his main asset was his throwing.

David became an All-American player in 1974 and still holds many Nebraska passing records, including most yards in a single game (297), season (2,074), and career (5,035).

Even though I worked with him closely for three or four years and we had a good relationship, I never felt I got to know him well personally. David had a soft, handsome appearance, capped with long, wavy, dark hair. He kept people at arm's length. He was polite to a fault, a very cordial person. He never raised his voice, never got angry. So we never had any conflict, and I think that kept us from getting to know each other as well as we might have.

It's difficult, however, to get close to any player. Maybe a basketball coach can get close to his players because there are only ten or fifteen of them. But with such a large number of players—more than a hundred on our team each year—it's harder. I purposefully try not to get too chummy. With six or seven quarterbacks on the team, for example, I can't show favoritism to one.

If a player is having a problem, I may have a talk with him to work things out, and this will allow me to get to know him better. But David's mood never changed. He always had a sunny disposition, even when he was hurt or had a bad game, so we never had such a conversation. In responding to his consistently positive outward attitude, I wasn't always sure I was addressing his real emotions.

David has survived in pro football for a number of years even though he's not been a starter. He has graduated from college and is doing some television and real estate work, and I'm sure he will be successful in whatever he does. He's that kind of person, quietly successful.

Vince Ferragamo was recruited by us out of high school in 1972, but his interest in Nebraska was casual. Eventually his decision came down to Stanford and California.

He and his parents signed a letter-of-intent with Stanford and put it in the mail. But his brother, who was his coach in high school and was more partial to California, talked Vince into going down to the post office and having them open the mail box to get the letter out. Then they submitted a letter-of-intent to California. I guess there was some question for a while as to whom he had really signed with, but eventually the letter with California stood up and he enrolled there.

Vince played at California under Mike White in 1972 and 1973. He and Steve Bartkowski played as freshmen and sophomores. I don't know whether Bartkowski was getting the upper hand or what, but Vince decided to leave and called to let me know he was interested in coming to Nebraska. He expressed a desire to play in an environment where there was more interest in football—and that meant Nebraska. Mike White gave him a release and he transferred. Of course he had to sit out a year here. And that made Vince the victim of an unfortunate situation.

When he arrived at Nebraska in 1974, he worked with our scouting team the whole fall. We had always taken scout team players to bowl games, so I took Vince along that year to the Sugar Bowl. We were on national television, and somebody from the West Coast was doing sideline work with a microphone and camera. He recognized Vince—his name was on the back of his jersey—and he interviewed Vince during the game. Of course there was absolutely no thought of playing Vince because we knew he was ineligible. But there were people who knew the rules who saw the interview and promptly turned us in to the NCAA. The rules stated that a player who is not eligible to play in the game can't make a bowl trip. The bowl trip constituted an illegal award to the player.

So we got called on the carpet by the NCAA, and I went to Kansas City and met with the infractions committee on two different occasions. Subsequently we turned ourselves in on two or three other players who had gone to bowl games that year or in previous years and who were similarly ineligible. We just had not been aware of the rule. The committee finally ruled Vince would be ineligible for play in the first game of the following year.

I told the committee that was unfair, that they should punish me or the university because I had been negligent. Vince had gone along simply because I had told him to come. There was no way he could have known the rule. Actually I didn't know it either, but at least I was in a position where I *should* have known it. They didn't buy that.

So Vince didn't start the first game of 1975. Terry Luck did. Terry played well, so it was about three games into Vince's junior year, when Terry got poked in the eye down at Oklahoma State and was seeing double, that we put Vince in. He played very well and started from then on. But controversy still dogged Vince and me.

We were 10-0 going into the Oklahoma game in 1975 when they beat us pretty soundly. We didn't play well as a team, and Vince threw several interceptions. Then in the practices prior to the Fiesta Bowl game, I thought Vince didn't practice as well as Terry Luck. Terry seemed to have a little more concentration and intensity. Of course, Vince was never a great practice player, so I started him in the Fiesta Bowl anyway.

But right off the bat Vince threw a ball to an Arizona State linebacker. Hit him right in the stomach. So I took Vince out and put Terry in. I thought Terry was playing pretty well, but we ended up losing the game 17-14. There was quite an uproar over my making the change. The fans had come to really appreciate Vince. He had serious dark eyes, deeply inset beneath bushy eyebrows. He was quite handsome and a very talented player. But I thought Terry, under the circumstances and from what I had seen in practice, deserved the chance to play that last game. He was a senior, a captain, and had battled back from two knee operations.

Vince survived that whole thing and I did too, and in 1976 he had a great season. He was named an All-American and also an Academic All-American.

Vince is really a nice person, and we remain good friends. He studied very hard and was admitted to medical school after his career at Nebraska. He combined football and medical school for two years but, somewhat like me, couldn't straddle the fence forever and has concentrated on professional football the past few years. I hope he finishes medical school some day.

Tagge, Humm, and Ferragamo were fine quarterbacks on winning teams. But they weren't real good runners, and we were consistently having trouble with Oklahoma.

Not only did we lose six straight to Oklahoma before 1978, but in 1979 Oklahoma was the spoiler *twice*—in the Orange Bowl, of course, on January 1, and then again November 24. We were undefeated and untied and had the Big Eight title and Orange Bowl trip on the line as we traveled to Norman for the November clash.

We held a 7-3 lead at half. But Billy Sims was superb, rushing for 247 yards against our number-one-ranked defense, and Oklahoma rallied for two touchdowns.

Our last score was on the "Fumblerooski," unveiled here for the first time but used occasionally since (including the 1984 Orange Bowl). After the snap the quarterback sets the ball on the ground for the offensive guard to pick up. The idea of leaving the ball on the ground sounds dangerous, but we practice it regularly and it's almost always successful. In this case, however, the play was too little, too late—a fifteen-yard scoring run by Randy Schleusener leaving us on the short end of a 17-14 final score.

We went on to the Cotton Bowl, losing to Houston by the same score.

Oklahoma thwarted our Big Eight championship hopes again in 1980. This time we took a blemish into the game, an 18-14 loss to Florida State in the fourth game of the season. That was it until— Oklahoma.

We jumped off to a 10-0 lead against the Sooners but fell behind 14-10 at the half. That score stood after three quarters as we held Oklahoma to just seven yards of offense since halftime.

We finally scored with about three minutes remaining, but the Sooners stormed back for the winning score with less than a minute on the clock. We had 390 yards to Oklahoma's 275, but they went to the Orange Bowl and we to the Sun Bowl, where we beat Mississippi State 31-17.

As time went on, I began to realize the biggest difference between our football team and Oklahoma was that they had speed at quarterback. They would run the wishbone and almost always had somebody at quarterback who could run a 4.6 forty or better and beat us running the ball. They generally had a running back with All-American capability—whether it be Joe Washington, Elvis Peacock, or Billy Sims—but they had talented quarterbacks who also could take the ball and run off with it and beat anybody. Even though we had a play defensed pretty well, if one guy missed the tackle it was all over.

Meanwhile we were playing running backs who were good, tough, steady, hardworking people like Tony Davis, who probably ran a 4.7 forty, and John O'Leary at 4.65. They could get ten yards, but they weren't going to get sixty. And we had quarterbacks who could throw the ball, but didn't have a lot of mobility.

There were years when I felt throughout the whole season that we were more consistent than Oklahoma. We had fewer turnovers, a better offensive or defensive line, better linebackers. But one or two big-play individuals would make the difference for them. So it was out of frustration that I began to realize that in order to compete with them, we were going to have to get game-breakers, including quarterbacks who could run better.

We don't try to make a sprint-out quarterback out of a drop-back quarterback or a fancy-dan runner out of a straight-ahead runner. We try to *recruit* those abilities.

Now we seldom recruit a quarterback who can't run 4.7 or better. And we also really intensified our efforts to recruit great running backs. We go all around the country to pick out the five, six, or seven best running backs we know of and figure we need to get one of them if possible. Of course, they're the toughest people to come by.

There's a tremendous competition for players like Mike Rozier and Roger Craig who were a cut above what we'd had the previous nine or ten years in terms of pure running ability, but with Rozier and Craig we got over the hump and were no longer behind Oklahoma in terms of talent in the running back position. In fact, for two or three years we had more talented runners than they did, we got a quarterback who was more talented than their quarterback, and things swung our way in 1981, 1982, and 1983. We beat Oklahoma three straight times.

We were able to win because we had the right personnel. We had, above all, a quarterback named Turner Gill.

Chapter Eleven

The Ideal Athlete

The first time I saw Turner Gill was at the 1980 Cotton Bowl game in which Nebraska was playing Houston. I remember Turner was wearing a big red and white jersey with "Houston" written on it, and I found out later his sister attended the University of Houston. I assumed he would be attending Houston the next fall.

As time went on, however, he seemed to be more and more interested in Nebraska, and we were able to persuade him and his parents that playing football at Nebraska would be more to his advantage than the Houston veer or Oklahoma wishbone. Playing at Nebraska would give him a chance to run an offense similar to what he had run in high school.

I spent a great deal of time personally recruiting Turner, but our defensive coordinator, Lance Van Zandt, really did most of the work. Turner needed quite a bit of confidence in me to come to Nebraska from Fort Worth, Texas, because he was hearing from other coaches that Nebraska had never had a black quarterback. "You'll never be given a chance," they'd say. "Nebraska won't play a black quarterback. You'll be recruited there and moved to receiver or defensive back."

When you're a high school senior and you've only seen a coach from far away a couple of times, it's difficult to know if you can trust him. And of course, a look at the history book proved we hadn't had a black quarterback who had played any appreciable time. In fact, only one or two black quarterbacks—period. Actually, none of them had the ability to start, but it was still used against us in recruiting.

I assured Turner we wanted him to be a quarterback. I got him to believe he'd be given a fair shake, and somehow he trusted me.

Of course, I didn't treat Turner differently from any other player when he arrived at Nebraska, but he had tremendous ability and we used him in ways—option football, play-action passes—that allowed him to be the best player he could be.

At times, however, Turner was the victim of our success because we moved the ball so well. We were running the ball so easily that he didn't need to throw very much. We averaged over seven yards on first down, so it was usually second down and three and we didn't face many situations where we had to pass. In many games, we were ahead by forty or fifty points at the start of the fourth quarter, so having him in there passing was both foolish (because he might get injured), and an insult to the opponent (contrary to some critics, I'm really concerned for the opponent in lopsided games).

So Turner averaged only fourteen or fifteen passes a game, which always kept him out of the NCAA passing statistics because of insufficient passing attempts. It also hurt his chances to be an All-American. But in terms of an all-around contribution to a football team—running, not turning the ball over, making the big plays—Turner Gill was the best. We lost only two games with Turner at quarterback, 27-24 to Penn State in 1982 (when they were national champions) and 31-30 to Miami in the 1984 Orange Bowl (when *they* were national champions).

Turner was the ideal athlete. He had good speed, a very strong arm, good hands, and durability. His main asset, however, was his personality. He had great confidence, poise, and leadership. These attributes clearly set him apart.

We almost lost Turner in mid-career. In the next-to-last regular season game of 1981, against Iowa State, Turner received a severe bruise in his left calf. He was limping, but said he could continue to play, and he did play well for another ten minutes until we had the game under control.

I didn't think much of the injury, and neither did anyone else until he called the doctor later that night and complained that he was experiencing a lot of pain and his toes were numb. The doctors operated on him that night to relieve pressure on the nerve controlling movement in his foot. At the time the doctors thought he might be able to play the next week against Oklahoma. But he couldn't play. He had lost all sensation and movement in his foot and ankle. Fortunately Mark Mauer, our senior quarterback, had a great game and we beat Oklahoma handily.

We were still certain, however, that Turner would be fine for the Orange Bowl game with Clemson in six weeks. He wasn't fine. The bowl game came and went. Mark Mauer played quarterback, but was hampered by a rotator cuff torn in practice. He couldn't put much on the ball, and Clemson beat us by one touchdown in a game for the national championship. It was a great disappointment, but even more disappointing was that there had been no change in Turner's leg after nearly two months.

Nobody said the words, but everybody thought about it: *Turner might never play anything again.*

He really preferred baseball to football and was hoping to have a career in the major leagues if things didn't work out in football. He thought he was too short to play pro football, but I didn't.

Over the next few months the nerve regenerated and he slowly regained movement—first in a toe, then in the foot, and finally in the ankle. By spring practice he could run plays, but not scrimmage. His foot still dragged a little. By the end of the summer, however, he was back to full speed with just a little weakness in the ankle, and he was able to play again.

The injury caused him to take a hard look at his life and where it was going, and I know it had an impact on his spiritual life. Adversity has a way of calling forth those qualities within us that are most enduring and are ultimately most important.

I was probably closer to Turner than to any other player I have coached. Partly it was because of the injury, but even more it grew out of his having to trust me to treat him fairly when people were telling him that I wouldn't because he was black. He was even told that the people of Nebraska weren't "ready" for a black quarterback. The first black played for Nebraska in the 1890s, and Turner was being told by people whose teams were segregated as recently as the 1950s that he wouldn't get a fair chance at Nebraska. It was hard to take.

I was honored to be a groomsman in his wedding in December of 1984.

Chapter Twelve

The Linemen

America gives much attention to the Heisman Trophy winners, but it's a mistake to claim that award goes to the *best* college football player each year. It goes to *one* of the best *offensive* players who *throws, catches,* or *runs* with the ball. It virtually ignores the great linemen who make possible many of the fine performances by quarterbacks, receivers, and running backs.

Nebraska has a tradition of producing top college linemen—people such as Dave Rimington and Dean Steinkuhler, back-to-back winners of the Lombardi Trophy, which is symbolic of the best collegiate lineman of the year. Both spectacular linemen, Dave and Dean present a study in sharp contrasts.

Dave came to us from Nebraska's largest town, Omaha, while Dean came from little Burr, Nebraska—population 110—where he had played eight-man football for Sterling High School. Dave's promise was well-publicized, while Dean was unknown and more of a question mark. Dave received a lot of attention early in his career, while Dean labored in Dave's shadow until his senior year.

Dave was quite outgoing and seemed to enjoy meeting with the press and being not only the center of our offensive line but also the center of attention. On the other hand, Dean had a tendency to stay in the background.

Dave Rimington was a very heavily recruited player before his graduation from Omaha South High School. He took his five allowed recruiting visits but assured me before he began his visits that he would attend Nebraska. Nevertheless, we certainly were concerned as Dave flew around the country visiting a different school each week. But each week he would return from the visit and let us know he was still thinking Nebraska.

In the Nebraska Shrine Bowl, a high school all-star game played the summer after he signed with us, Dave suffered a knee injury that was later found to be more severe than we'd first assumed. He had torn a cruciate ligament, and at the time we didn't have the medical technology to repair the injury. Therefore, Dave played his four years of football at Nebraska with the ligament injury, and this caused him a lot of pain at times.

To watch him play, however, you would have never known he had the problem. He was exceptionally quick off the ball, very strong, and exceptionally intelligent. He was able to do about as many things at offensive center as you would ever hope to see. He was able to reach-block a man over either guard as well as get out very quickly on a middle linebacker. And, of course, he was usually able to dominate anyone who played on his nose and went one-on-one with him.

Dave considered going into pro football after the 1982 Orange Bowl game with Clemson at the conclusion of his junior year. We were relieved when he decided to come back and play his last year at Nebraska, and I think it paid off for him. He had his greatest year and won both the Lombardi and Outland trophies—a tremendous accomplishment.

Dean Steinkuhler came to Nebraska by a very different route. He played fullback and was also in the line for Sterling High. For some reason he wasn't thought to be a good enough player by the coaches in his eight-man football league to make the All-Conference team.

He had no reputation as a graduating senior, and there was practically nothing in the way of game films by which to evaluate his high school play. Therefore, we had little to go on, and almost all we knew of Dean came as he participated in our football camp the summer before his senior year. Dean showed good speed and agility and we liked his attitude, so we offered him a scholarship.

When he came to Nebraska, Dean only weighed 215 pounds, but he worked very hard in the weight room and spent a year as a red-shirt. Both of these factors enabled him to progress further physically. Eventually he was able to play at about 270 pounds and run a forty-yard dash in under 4.7.

In the 1984 Orange Bowl game, when we were trailing 17-0, we ran the guard-around play on a third and five situation—the "Fumble-rooski" I mentioned earlier. The center snapped the ball to Turner Gill, who intentionally dropped the ball on the ground. Turner then circled around the right end as though he had the ball, and Dean, from his right guard spot, scooped up the ball and ran around the left end on a naked reverse. Dean made it all the way into the end-zone from twenty yards out, scoring our first touchdown of the game. It was a big play. It got us on the scoreboard and we began to develop some offensive momentum.

Eventually, the contrasts between the backgrounds and personalities of Dave and Dean gave way to similarities as each performed brilliantly for us. They both received many honors, and became first-round draft choices.

After being red-shirted as a freshman in 1978, Dave played four straight years on the varsity squad—three as a starter, two as the Outland Trophy winner, and one as the Lombardi Trophy winner. In addition to being quick he was powerful—one of the strongest players ever at Nebraska. He could bench press 425 pounds. And his intelligence extended beyond the playing field into the classroom. He was a two-time Academic All-American as well as an outstanding offensive center. In 1983 he was drafted in the first round by the Cincinnati Bengals.

Dean was red-shirted, too, and added fifty pounds to his body and 125 pounds to his bench press through hard work early in his career. He learned to be as consistent a performer as any lineman Nebraska has ever had. He started at offensive guard for three seasons, won both the Outland and Lombardi trophies as a senior in 1983, and was drafted in the first round by the Houston Oilers in 1984. It was a source of great pride to us when Dean was given the Outland and Lombardi Trophies only one year after Dave had received the same honors. We knew Dean was deserving but felt his attending the same school as Dave would make it less likely the voters would see fit to award him these trophies.

Dave Rimington and Dean Steinkuhler were both a cut above the average college lineman, but there have been many committed, disciplined players who have labored in the trenches at Nebraska and the nation's other schools to protect passers and pave the way for exciting runners. Two of the best of these runners also form a significant chapter in my life.

Chapter Thirteen

The Heisman Trophy Winners

Nebraska has had two Heisman Trophy winners in its celebrated football tradition. I've observed both—Johnny Rodgers in 1972 and Mike Rozier in 1983. Both made headlines off the field as well as on.

The first I heard about Johnny Rodgers was that he was one of two high school players in Omaha—small, quick players—over whom there was some debate. "Who's better? Can *either* make it at all in spite of his size?"

We were only going to take one of the two, and finally it was decided we would recruit Johnny over the other player. It's amazing that with his ability and what he later accomplished, we would debate whether to recruit him or not. Johnny later said that he had wanted to go to the University of Southern California, but fortunately USC didn't recruit him and he signed with Nebraska.

In his first year, Johnny did a lot of exciting things for the freshman team, but I didn't really sense how good he was going to be. In the spring of his freshman year I got a good, close look at him because I was working with the varsity receivers and he was a wingback—a combination receiver and running back. Only then did I begin to sense his ability.

Looking back now, I can say Johnny was probably the best broken-field runner I've ever been associated with and one of the greatest competitors I've observed. But he also had ulcers. There were a few times when he had to go to the student health center because he was bleeding internally. I know he was really hurting. This usually happened as the season wore on. He gave the impression that nothing bothered him, but I'm sure his drive to succeed intensified his stomach problems.

Often on Monday and sometimes on Tuesday he didn't practice, and we were always concerned the other players might feel Johnny was loafing. But they never gave him a problem. He almost always had legitimate injuries because he took quite a beating during games. He played hard even though he wasn't very big. Usually by Wednesday he was ready to practice. He would do what he had to do to get himself ready to play. Then, come Saturday, he was a tremendous competitor and gave 100 percent. He was a great game player.

In his senior year, Johnny set a goal of winning the Heisman Trophy, so he wanted the football. One game he wasn't getting the ball very much, so he grabbed the headphones and talked to me up in the press box and told me he wanted the ball more often. I said, "Johnny, I can't guarantee we can give it to you! I can call a pass pattern, but we can't throw to you if you're covered and another receiver is open."

He was late to practice occasionally, and we made him run just like everyone else. I usually ran with him because I always ran after practice anyway. Sometimes he complained to Coach Devaney about it, but we tried to be diligent in making sure the rules applied to him just as to all the other players. We knew on Saturday he would play hard, but we didn't want anybody to feel he was getting off the hook.

In the spring of his freshman year, Johnny robbed a gas station. The incident didn't come to light until over a year later. Somebody who had known about the incident finally reported it to the police, and Johnny was arrested. I went down to the jail and helped get him out. We talked about it, and at first he said he hadn't done it. I believed him. Then he said it was a prank. I knew Johnny got in some scrapes, but armed robbery wasn't his style. The whole episode was out of character.

Whatever the reason, the incident made quite a few waves, and Bob had to decide what to do about it. He chose to play Johnny in his senior year; there was some pressure not to.

I really felt something ought to be done to Johnny. I thought he should sit out a year or at least be suspended for some games. But Bob noted it was Johnny's first offense and that it had occurred almost two years earlier. He said, "It won't do him any good not to play." Bob may have been rationalizing a little, but he was probably right in not taking any disciplinary action under the circumstances. Johnny went on to have a great senior season and he won the Heisman Trophy.

Johnny left Nebraska holding just about every pass receiving record for the school. Seven of those records still stand, including most catches and yards in a season (55 and 942) and most catches and yards in a career (143 and 2,474). He also still holds three kick-off return records and all ten punt-return marks kept by the school.

His ability to return punts was the greatest I have ever seen. He could extricate himself from seemingly impossible situations—sometimes with a lateral move, sometimes with strength, sometimes with acceleration. He had 5,586 all-purpose yards (rushing, receiving, returns), which is still a career-best at Nebraska. More importantly, he was the key player in our 1970 and 1971 national championships as he was the "difference maker" in most of our big games.

Nineteen-eighty was a very important year in Nebraska football, because it was the year we recruited three of the most outstanding skill players I've known—Turner Gill, Irving Fryar, and Mike Rozier—given the name "The Triplets" by some in the media.

I've already mentioned the obstacles we had to overcome to attract Turner to Nebraska. Irving and Mike arrived in Lincoln by very different routes. They were both from New Jersey, and both were late additions to our recruiting efforts.

Frank Solich, one of our assistant coaches, had been told Irving Fryar was a great athlete. However, in looking at Irving's films, it was very difficult to see him doing much. He played tight end most of the time and didn't catch the ball a great deal. The films were also difficult to evaluate because they weren't of good quality. But we went ahead and offered Irving a scholarship simply because we'd heard he had good speed and good athletic ability. At the time, we weren't even sure what position he would be able to play. That's how scientific recruiting is sometimes. He ended up as the NFL's top draft pick in 1984.

Mike Rozier was also noticed by Frank about the same time. He was watching films of a player whose team was playing against Mike's team, and Frank kept noticing Mike on the film. Frank brought the films back to Lincoln, and we looked at the films together. We decided Mike was definitely an outstanding back, even though he wasn't receiving a great deal of attention. Mike played fullback on a wishbone team and didn't get the ball much, but when he did, he really made things happen.

During Mike's senior year of high school, the teachers in his home town of Camden, New Jersey, went on strike. This made it very difficult for him to raise his grade-point level to meet NCAA minimum standards. He was slightly under a 2.0 average, and he needed to have a good second semester in order to reach a 2.0. Largely because of the school strike, he came up just short academically and couldn't qualify for a scholarship.

We called Coffeyville Junior College and asked Dick Foster, the coach there, if he would take Mike for a year in hopes that Mike would be able to raise his grades and then enter the University of Nebraska. Dick was in the habit of getting players and releasing them after only one year, and he told us he could use a great running back and would be delighted to have Mike.

Mike consented to go to Coffeyville and put in a rather difficult year there, as Coffeyville is a small Kansas community very different from Camden. But he played on a good football team and did get his grades up. I can recall flying down to the Beef Bowl game in Garden City, Kansas, to watch Coffeyville play a junior college team from Arizona in late November. Mike played reasonably well but wasn't outstanding in the game. It was very cold and Coffeyville was running the wishbone, so Mike didn't get to do some of the things in that game that he later showed.

After that season we had to recruit Mike all over again. He was now very much in demand and was promised some illegal inducements. But he appreciated that we had been interested in him earlier when he hadn't been heavily recruited and had grade problems, and he maintained a sense of loyalty to Nebraska.

In fall camp of 1981, Mike got his first chance to be in a Nebraska uniform, and he exceeded all expectations. There were two or three early scrimmages where he ran right through our first defense. This was made even more impressive because he was running behind our second-team offensive line. He learned our system quickly, but because he was unfamiliar with some of the plays, he played only sparingly in the first two or three games. We had another great running back that year in Roger Craig, so Mike and Roger shared time. Mike became a little more prominent as the season went along as Roger was hampered by some minor injuries. Both Mike and Roger ended up with more than a thousand yards rushing in the 1981 season, and Mike certainly showed the promise that would later make him an All-American and a Heisman Trophy winner.

The game against Missouri in 1982 was the most remarkable performance Mike ever gave. In the game prior to Missouri he had sustained a severe hip pointer—an injury that causes great pain anytime you cough, twist, or run. He hadn't been able to practice much all week and couldn't even get down in a three-point-stance because of the pain. The doctors didn't think he would be able to play, so we had him on the sideline during the first quarter. Mike kept coming up and pestering the backfield coach and then me saying he was ready to play, so we put him in at the start of the second quarter since we weren't doing very well. He proceeded to have a great game in spite of the pain—139 yards rushing in seventeen attempts, and three pass receptions for twenty-four yards. Key to our win was an outstanding run Mike made late in the game. He started to his left, cut back through the middle of the line, and was hit very hard and reinjured when he was brought down at the Missouri two yard line. We scored from there and iced the win. That game will always stick in my memory as one of the most courageous individual performances I've ever seen.

Mike was blessed with probably the best overall set of abilities I've ever seen in a running back. He weighed approximately 210 pounds, was built low to the ground, and had great balance and strength that made him a terrific inside runner. He also had the speed, acceleration, and elusiveness to run to the outside. In addition to these abilities, he could catch the ball very well, was a good passer, and a great blocker. He would often hustle downfield and throw tremendous blocks when the fullback or quarterback carried the ball—something very rare for a great runner.

He was just a tremendous, natural, all-around athlete and was especially effective on game day. He wasn't overly fond of the weight room and at times didn't like long hard practices, but when the whistle blew he was always ready to play and give every ounce of effort he had to offer. He had a good team perspective and was always encouraging the offensive line, as he understood the importance of their role in whatever success he enjoyed. Mike's senior season was his best because he rushed for over two thousand yards, won the Heisman Trophy, and was a consensus All-American.

Then Mike signed a pro contract only hours after the Orange Bowl game of 1984. The fact that he signed so quickly with the Pittsburgh Maulers of the United States Football League caused members of the press to be very suspicious that he had taken money from an agent or been involved with an agent in some other way prior to the completion of his eligibility. Since it would be very hard to put together a deal such as he had with the Maulers in only hours, it was assumed somebody had been working on this for some time.

The press wouldn't leave Mike alone, and the next months were difficult for him because he was continually subjected to questioning about his possible involvement with an agent prior to the completion of the season. Eventually—it was several months later—Mike admitted that he had received a loan the summer before his senior year from a Los Angeles businessman. He told me he hadn't understood at the time that the loan in any way tied him to an agent. He believed it was simply a loan that he would be able to pay back at the conclusion of the football season.

According to what Mike has told me, he had been approached initially back in New Jersey by a former player from the Pittsburgh Steelers whom Mike knew and the Los Angeles businessman, whom he'd never met. Ironically, when they first approached Mike they were really trying to find Irving Fryar.

Mike used the money to lease a car in Omaha. When I saw him driving a 1979 Buick Riviera, I asked him how he got the money for it. "Back home," he said. I checked into the leasing agreement and found it to be legitimate, but it has turned out to cost Mike a lot more than he imagined then.

Mike told me that prior to his participation in the 1984 Orange Bowl an agent approached him in Miami about letting him represent Mike. The agent maintained that the loan money had come from him and that if Mike didn't follow through and let the agent represent him, Mike might have to give back his Heisman Trophy and Nebraska might have to forfeit the twelve games that we had won that season. Mike told me later he believed there was something to the threats of having to relinquish the Heisman Trophy and of having jeopardized the games we'd won, so he let the agent go ahead and negotiate his contract. It's my understanding that Mike and his family dismissed the agent only a few weeks later, as they had not appreciated the way the whole thing was handled. Obviously it was a rushed situation, and not all the options available to Mike were explored.

I was upset with this whole affair because I felt that, looking back, it might have affected his preparation for the Orange Bowl. It certainly made the next year of Mike's life very difficult. He was continually on the defensive with the press. Eventually when the Pittsburgh Maulers folded and Mike tried to hook on with other teams, management would ask me questions about his character. They wondered if they should go ahead and try to sign Mike, which meant picking up the large contract he carried with him. Subsequently Mike bought out part of the contract from the Pittsburgh Maulers' owner and renegotiated his own deal with the Jacksonville Bulls of the USFL.

The events of Mike's senior year illustrate how professional agents are now infringing on college football more than ever. There are numerous agents who are quite reputable and who will wait until the player's senior season is over before they attempt to enter into negotiations with him. On the other hand, there are a few agents who feel they need to have an edge. They will attempt to contact the player several months, or even sometimes a year or two, before his senior year and try in some way to obligate that player to them so that they might have leverage in representing him when it's time for him to turn professional.

In response to all these pressures college athletes face today, we have set up a class at Nebraska to educate our players regarding NCAA and NFL rules on contracts. We also discuss the selection of an agent, and we try to spend some time talking about investments. We hope this educational procedure will help players avoid some of the problems Mike had. Mike himself has been active in talking to some of our players about his situation in the hope that they might profit from his unfortunate experience.

Some of the problems Mike had in terms of feeling he needed extra money during his last year may relate to changes that the NCAA scholarship has undergone in recent years. When the grant-in-aid for an athlete was first initiated, the maximum grant included paying for room, board, books, tuition, fees, plus fifteen dollars a month for incidental expenses. A few years ago the fifteen dollars a month was eliminated, and many coaches feel this was a mistake. The fifteen dollars a month that was granted back in the late fifties and early sixties would now be worth more than fifty dollars a month with the inflation that has occurred since then, and certainly many players have difficulty coming up with any spending money.

It seems as though we demand more and more from the players and give them less and less return financially. The season has gone from a nine-game schedule a number of years ago to the current eleven-game schedule, and many of us have played schedules with twelve games by playing in Hawaii, Japan, or the Kickoff Classic in New Jersey, which are all games that do not count in the eleven-game schedule. Therefore, it's possible for a team to now play twelve regular season games plus a bowl game.

Also in the late sixties and early seventies, all of us in coaching began to realize that just having twenty days of spring football plus the regular practice in the fall wasn't going to be sufficient in terms of athletic development. Therefore, most schools now have rather sophisticated off-season programs that will take five, six, or seven weeks of a player's time prior to spring football. Intensive weightlifting, agility, and running programs are commonplace. In addition, in order to maintain pace, most players must spend a substantial amount of time working out in the summer months. Therefore, being a major college athlete involves some form of preparation almost year-round.

NCAA rules, however, prohibit a player from working during the school year except during vacation periods. The idea is to protect the student athlete. But the result is that a student who has a good part-time job and who is paying his way through school will often be as well off financially—in some ways better off—as a player on a full scholarship. Further, a player who isn't able to have a summer job because of summer school will usually have to rely heavily on financial help from home, and there are some athletes whose families simply cannot afford to help them at all. Therefore, many coaches (myself included) advocate adding fifty dollars a month spending money to the basic amount of the scholarship.

In addition, athletes who have a great deal of need in their families can qualify for federal Pell Grants that would give them up to $1,800 a year in government aid. Current NCAA rules, however, allow an athlete to keep only $900 of the Pell Grant over and above the amount of the scholarship. These athletes who have demonstrated need should be allowed to keep the full $1,800 in addition to the amount of the basic NCAA scholarship. If these rule changes were made, a player would receive approximately $450 to $500 extra spending money on his grant-in-aid and could, conceivably, if there was sufficient need on the part of his family, have an extra $900 in Pell Grant money. This would make athletes less tempted to take illegal inducements.

Of course, there are always a few people who will succumb to the lure of illegal aid no matter what, but I believe that we are now asking a great deal more of our athletes and giving them a great deal less in return.

I like to remember Mike Rozier as the most prolific runner and scorer in Nebraska's rich football tradition. He holds eight Nebraska rushing records including most yards in a game (285), in a season (2,148), and in a career (4,780). He also holds four Nebraska scoring records including most points in a season (174) and in a career (312).

Finally, he received an award for being Nebraska's most popular player with the fans in 1983—an award I think he cherishes now more than ever.

Chapter Fourteen

The Booker Brown Affair

W e certainly would have liked to play in the 1985 Orange Bowl for the national championship, but after three consecutive years in Miami, many of us were looking forward to the change to the Sugar Bowl and New Orleans against Louisiana State University.

We flew to New Orleans on Christmas Day, arriving early in the afternoon at the Hilton Hotel on the banks of the Mississippi River. We had Christmas dinner as a team before unpacking and settling in.

The following day I rose early to set the practice schedule. I met with the quarterbacks at 9:30 and the full team at 10:00. Brunch was at 11:00, and our first practice at the New Orleans Saints' practice area was from 2:30–4:30. Practice was hard because of the 75° heat and high humidity—a big change from the cold that had driven us to inside workouts back in Lincoln.

When I returned to the hotel from practice, I had a message to return a telephone call to a Los Angeles newspaper reporter, so I called. The reporter said a man named Booker Brown, whom I had recruited twelve years earlier, had written a letter to the *Los Angeles Herald Examiner*. She read me his charges—that I had gotten him a

date, given him three hundred dollars cash in 1972 when he visited
Nebraska, had allowed him to drive my car to Omaha, had guaranteed
he would receive one thousand dollars if he wanted to sell his season
football tickets (given to all team members for their families), had
promised his mother six free trips to Nebraska at university expense,
and had promised him a car.

At first I couldn't even remember Booker Brown and was totally
dumbfounded by the whole matter. The writer then told me that
Booker had been a junior college offensive lineman from Santa Bar-
bara City College. With this additional information I remembered a
Booker Brown whom I had recruited in the early seventies, but I was
still amazed at the charges and told her so. I also told her the charges
were totally untrue.

After hanging up the phone, I sat on the bed trying to understand
why someone would make charges like this, especially after so many
years had elapsed. I got up and wandered randomly around the room,
pausing several times to stare out the window at the lights of New Orleans.

Finally it occurred to me that I had recently made negative statements about an agent from southern California, statements that had
appeared on national television. I wondered almost out loud, *Maybe
that agent is involved.*

I crossed the room, picked up the phone, and called the reporter
back. I told her of my suspicion that the agent—the same person
who'd been involved in Mike Rozier's loan situation—might, in some
way, be connected to the charges by Booker Brown. "You might want
to find out if Booker Brown was represented by this agent when he
was a player." She said she'd check it out, and we hung up.

My initial reaction was to be very angry about all this, and I was also
rather depressed. *We've spent a lot of time and effort to run a program
that would be without blemish as far as NCAA violations are concerned*, I thought, *and now this.*

Many people believe there is very little integrity in college athletics,
and I feared Brown's charges would be accepted by some and substantiate their worst beliefs about me, Nebraska, and college athletics
in general. It was the type of situation that would be hard to defend
against.

The next morning, Thursday, December 27, I called the Pendleton Detective Agency in New Orleans and tried to set up an immediate polygraph test. They told me they wouldn't be able to get me in until Friday. This disturbed me because I was in a frame of mind to take some kind of immediate action, even though I wasn't exactly sure what I wanted to do.

The Pendleton Agency was recommended by the New Orleans Chief of Police and other law enforcement officials. They were supposed to be very competent and reliable in administering polygraph examinations, so I made the appointment for Friday with their chief examiner. It was a strange turn of events to feel compelled to defend myself in this way. And it was only four days before the Sugar Bowl.

On Thursday I received many phone calls from reporters wanting to know about the allegations, and I also asked a couple of attorneys for their advice. They counseled me against taking a polygraph test because they felt that even though I was innocent, the test might prove to be inconclusive, and this could be more damaging than just letting the matter ride. However, in my state of mind, I was determined to attempt to do anything I could to clear my name and the University of Nebraska. So I felt compelled to take the test on Friday morning.

As I drove to the Pendleton Agency, I was apprehensive about the polygraph. I know quite a bit about how the autonomic nervous system works, and I realized I was emotionally upset enough about the whole issue that there would be some chance my test would not be very conclusive. I felt awkward as I met the Pendleton representatives, but after conferring with the polygrapher for approximately forty-five minutes, we were able to get the questions worded in a manner that I felt would be most appropriate. I expanded the questions to cover all my recruiting over twenty-three years and not just Booker Brown, because if there were further charges forthcoming, it would save me the trouble of having to go through the process again.

"Since your employment with the University of Nebraska, have you ever promised a prospective athlete that you had arranged for the sale of that athlete's game tickets?" the examiner asked.

"No," I responded.

"Did you ever give Booker Brown three hundred dollars when he visited the University Nebraska in 1972?"

Again the answer was no.

"Since your employment with the University of Nebraska, have you ever promised a prospective athlete a car as an inducement to attend the University of Nebraska?"

Once again the answer was no.

"Since your employment with the University of Nebraska, have you ever promised to provide any free transportation for an athlete or his relatives as an inducement to attend the University of Nebraska?"

The answer was no.

I wasn't asked and didn't answer the charge about getting Brown a date, as there was nothing wrong with that. My ability to obtain dates would have been almost negligible anyway, even if I had wanted to arrange something like that. The player who hosted Brown might have gotten him a date.

I also wasn't asked and didn't respond to the charge that Brown had driven my car to Omaha. When I first started recruiting, I would occasionally let the student-host use my car if he didn't have one. It was legal then. When the rules changed, I followed the rules as I became aware of them. If Brown drove my car, it was because a host-player let him drive it. I have no recollection of lending my car out when he visited, however.

The test was over in sixty minutes, and I was excused from the examination room. I paced and fidgeted for approximately thirty minutes, alone with my worries, while the polygrapher went through the results. When he came in the room where I waited, I stopped pacing in my tracks and stood erect. "Coach Osborne," he said, "I'm convinced you are telling the truth on all accounts."

I breathed a sigh of relief, asked for a copy of the test results, and thanked him and departed. I was able to concentrate a little better on practice that afternoon. I must admit that during the preceding two days my mind at times had not been focusing on football as well as it should have been.

That evening at about 9:00, I was sitting in my room talking to Nancy about the unusual events of the day when the phone rang, and the unusual gave way to the absurd. It was Booker Brown.

Brown told me he had taken a polygraph test that day too, and had passed it. He also mentioned he had seen a television show in which I had claimed to be ethical and had made negative comments about his former agent. He said, "I know you're not an ethical person! That's why I've come forward with these charges after twelve years. You drove a wedge between me and my mother. I wanted to go to USC, but my mother wanted me to go to Nebraska because of the trips you promised her."

At that point I suggested his agent might possibly be behind all this, and Brown said the agent was with him. Then the agent got on the phone and, indeed, he was the man I suspected.

He said something about Brown having passed the lie detector test "with flying colors." It sounded as if he thought he had me. Then he went into a discussion in which he said he wanted a "key to the front door" to talk to and recruit Nebraska athletes so that he might be their agent. I told him I would treat him like all other agents, which meant he could visit with our senior players but not until after our last regular season game. But he said he felt he'd have to come in during the summer.

"After all that's happened," I asked, "you want me to allow you access to our players in the summer?"

"Yes," he responded. "That's what I'm asking."

The agent mentioned a television show in which he debated another agent. Prior to that debate a film clip was shown of me saying I had advised our players not to deal with him. This had caught him off guard and had made him angry. Apparently Booker Brown had seen this in addition to hearing the agent's negative comments about me and my integrity, and this may have affected him.

In all fairness to the agent, I can understand his being angry over the television show. He had apparently agreed to appear on the show and debate various aspects of the agent business with another agent who had the reputation of being a "good guy." Apparently the producer of the show had obtained a short segment of a TV interview done by one of our local television stations in which I had said that I was surprised Mike Rozier had signed with whom he had, because he was the one agent I had told our players to stay away from. This agent had previously attempted to sign our players early, and at that time he was not certified by the NFL players association. I had made the statement to local writers and TV people out of genuine surprise over the whole matter and certainly had not intended to single out or embarrass the agent on the national program. It was unfair of the show's producer to use my statement as he did—it had the desired effect, however, in that it produced plenty of fireworks.

The telephone conversation, even though it was unexpected and depressing, really clarified things for me. It confirmed my suspicions that Booker Brown quite likely would not have come forth with a statement after twelve years, and certainly would not have taken the trouble to personally call newspapers in Omaha, Lincoln, and other points around the country to be sure they hadn't missed his statement about me, unless he had been prompted to do so. The phone call made the relationship between Booker Brown and the agent apparent.

I had been upset with this agent since he had gotten two of our players involved with him in the late seventies through the use of former Nebraska players. These two players were extricated from any involvement with him before their senior season. However, I could see that their eligibility would have been jeopardized had they continued to be involved with him. Then, of course, through some of his employees, he had managed to get Mike Rozier involved in the loan situation that hurt Mike's reputation.

Previously this agent had stated in a national magazine that he often had gotten clients by obligating them to him before their senior year. Obviously, this wasn't the kind of person I wanted to give the "key to the front door."

The next day, Saturday, December 29, I had a press conference at the Hyatt Regency Hotel in conjunction with the Sugar Bowl game. I spent about twenty minutes talking about the game and our football team and then was asked about the Booker Brown affair. At that time I presented the information that had been obtained in the polygraph test and also discussed the phone call from Brown and the agent. I discussed the matter with the reporters for over half an hour, trying to be very thorough in covering all possible questions so that I could put it behind me until after the game. I felt the matter had already taken a tremendous amount of time and energy away from my personal preparation for the game, and I hoped it wasn't hurting the team. It seemed the reporters were receptive and believed what I said, and I was relieved when the press conference was over.

I mentioned, in conjunction with the press conference, that the university was willing to back me in a legal action if it was deemed necessary to pursue such a course. This was an option we were considering in view of the damage to me personally but also in view of the damage that might have been done in regard to the overall integrity of our program and the university.

The Booker Brown affair points up the vulnerability of people in coaching and public life in general. I have been involved with well over one thousand recruits in the past twenty-three years, but only this one claims impropriety—and twelve years ago at that! But *this* accusation gets all the attention.

If the press is willing to give credibility to charges such as Booker Brown's, it seems quite possible for almost any coach to come under attack with little documented evidence to substantiate the claims. It is my feeling that credence should not be given to such allegations unless they have been substantiated in some significant way. It always appears as though subsequent denials and facts never get quite the same publicity or dissemination as the initial charges, which may be more sensational, do receive. I had asked the Los Angeles reporter who read Booker Brown's charges to me for Booker's phone number. She replied that this "wouldn't be fair to Booker." I then pointed out to her that unsubstantiated charges about me were being printed all over the country without much concern about "being fair."

Blatant cheating in recruiting—involving loans, cars, clothes, and cash—certainly exists in college athletics. The extent of this cheating varies from one part of the country to another and from year to year. My personal experience is that this type of serious cheating is not as common as the average fan would believe. The NCAA has greatly expanded its enforcement staff in recent years and is doing a reasonably good job of catching those who willfully and systematically defy the rules.

Unfortunately, there is another form of dishonesty in recruiting that is much more common. This is misrepresentation—for example, "promising" a player he will start or play a great deal right away, spreading rumors about other programs, and giving false impressions of the quality of one's own program.

After the press conference, we practiced in the Superdome for the first time. Although I was still angry, I felt much better having the press conference behind me. And the team had its best practice since arriving in New Orleans. The impressiveness of the Superdome seemed to jar the players out of their sluggishness. Or perhaps it was the bedchecks we'd been having the previous three nights. More sleep was probably helping.

We practiced in the Dome on Sunday and briefly again on Monday. Afterward the players were sent to a movie and the coaches attended a New Year's Eve dinner and dance at the hotel. Pete Fountain played and was very good, but I left the dance early to meet with the players when they returned from the movie.

New Year's Day was long. Night games are difficult because of the seemingly endless wait. In the morning we had meetings and worship services. In the afternoon I called recruits and watched the Cotton Bowl and portions of other games.

We seemed still to be waiting for our game to start during the first quarter and fell behind 3-0 with 4:36 remaining. At the end of the first quarter, LSU had six first downs to our one, and 125 total yards to our 28. Two minutes into the second quarter, LSU went out front 10-0.

Our only bright spot of the first half was a six-play, seventy-yard drive in a little over two minutes with Doug Dubose scoring on a thirty-one-yard screen pass and run. LSU blew a couple of scoring opportunities or the 10-7 score at half-time could have been much worse. LSU had 300 total yards in the first half, more than double our total.

I was angry and frustrated at half-time and yelled a bit in the locker room. We came out the second half and scored on our first possession—a long drive with senior quarterback Craig Sundberg keeping for the touchdown.

In the fourth quarter Sundberg hit Todd Frain for a twenty-three-yard touchdown off a bootleg, capping an eleven-play, eighty-yard drive. Two minutes later Sundberg tossed to Frain again for seventeen yards, pushing the score to 28-10 with the point after.

That's how it ended, capping a 10-2 season. Polls ranked us as high as second, as low as fourth, but most often third behind Brigham Young and Washington.

Craig Sundberg was named the game's most valuable player, which pleased me tremendously. Craig came to Nebraska at the same time as Turner Gill and red-shirted in order to have an opportunity to step out of Turner's shadow for a season. He had an up-and-down year in 1984 due to injury, but his hard work and perseverance paid off. His 10 for 15 passing performance, good for three touchdowns, plus another touchdown running, was a perfect end to the career of this fine young man.

Moreover, Craig had been sick with the flu until right before the game. He is a young man of strong faith, and he attributed his ability to progress from a weak, bedridden quarterback to most valuable player in the Sugar Bowl in just a few hours to God's grace. I hadn't thought Craig would be able to play when I saw him at the pre-game meal at 3:30 that afternoon and would have to say that his performance seemed truly miraculous.

When Craig had become ill, I had had a sinking feeling. Things hadn't gone well since the final game of the year against Oklahoma, and the bowl trip hadn't been exactly a piece of cake. It didn't look as though we would get things back on track either, as Craig was the quarterback we had prepared to start. Craig had waited five years to start and then had been replaced as starter at midseason. So this one last chance to start was very important to him. I personally believe that Craig's faith was a big factor in his performance. His being named the Sugar Bowl M.V.P. was beyond my best hopes.

In the end, doing what we knew how to do paid off in that game. We were aggressive, ran right at LSU, and wore them down. We had more experience and poise, and were the better team in the fourth quarter.

When all is said and done, I believe the integrity of our program will be vindicated and the Booker Brown affair will fade from most people's memories. The Sugar Bowl victory was sweet enough to allow me to forget about the matter for a while, but I'll never totally forget it or stop wondering why Brown said what he did and how much damage his unfounded allegations may have caused.

Chapter Fifteen

Slowing Down

I first noticed it while jogging in mid-December. It was during our preparation for the 1985 Sugar Bowl against LSU in New Orleans. I had an uncomfortable feeling in my chest. It wasn't really a pain, but rather a fullness or tightness that would hit me after I had run for about three quarters of a mile. Usually I could run through it, and by the end of three or four miles it was no longer very noticeable.

I thought it was a virus that would go away, but it got worse as the Sugar Bowl approached. There were a couple of occasions when I had planned to run three or four miles but actually ran only one or two because of the discomfort. The Sugar Bowl game came and went, and we plunged into recruiting full-speed. I continued with my daily running, usually alone, and was a little less uncomfortable than I had been in New Orleans.

One afternoon I ran with Nancy on an indoor track in Lincoln and noticed she seemed to be running faster than I could ever remember her running before! While I wasn't struggling, I was having to run fairly hard to keep up with her. This began to concern me.

The last straw came during a recruiting trip when I was running in San Diego with George Darlington, one of our coaches. George is a steady jogger but not very fast, and it bothered me that George was running at a pace that was about the same as mine. At the end of that five mile run, I decided I was going to make an appointment to have my heart checked when I returned to Lincoln.

So I called my cardiologist friend Walt Weaver from San Diego and asked if I could get an appointment. We were nearing the end of the recruiting period, and I thought it might take two or three weeks to get in to see him. To my surprise, Walt left word that he wanted to see me Friday afternoon when I flew back to Lincoln. He said he would wait in his office until I got there.

When I arrived in Lincoln I went straight to his office without stopping at home or the football office. Walt administered an electrocardiogram and, before putting me on the treadmill, called in his partner, Paul Jewitt. There was some concern in their voices.

I learned from Walt that both my resting and treadmill EKG were abnormal. "I believe it is important, Tom, that we insert a catheter in your heart and inject dye into the heart to determine exactly what's causing the change in the EKG from previous ones you've had." He scheduled me to do this procedure early Monday morning, February 4.

I drove home, put the car in the garage, and went straight to the bedroom without greeting Nancy, whom I hadn't seen for a week. This odd behavior wasn't overlooked by Nancy, and she didn't waste much time following me into the bedroom.

"What's wrong, Tom?"

"Nothing," I said, concentrating on my unpacking more than on Nancy.

"Oh, Tom. Yes there is. You're gone a week, come home, and go straight to the bedroom without saying hello? Something's wrong."

"Well, I've got a strange EKG," I deadpanned, finally looking at her.

"What do you mean a 'strange EKG'?"

"I stopped by Walt's office this afternoon when I got into town. I had the test. I'm scheduled for a catheterization on Monday. I wanted to have it done today, but I couldn't get in."

The quick and matter-of-fact nature of my decision didn't surprise Nancy. She's used to it. However, I could sense her concern, and I know she hadn't anticipated a problem with my health. Neither of us had.

That Saturday and Sunday I had a normal (hectic) recruiting weekend and felt fine, but the upcoming test was in the back of my mind. On Monday morning I checked into the hospital at 6:30, and by 7:30 they had started the catheterization procedure. A hollow, but very flexible catheter was inserted into my groin and up a vein into my heart. Walt maneuvered the catheter around and every few seconds would shoot some dye into various parts of the heart. A TV monitor clearly showed the arteries as the dye went through them in various areas of the heart. The first two or three shots appeared to me to be normal. Then, all of a sudden, there it was.

There was a definite narrowing in one of the arteries that showed just a thin stream of blood getting through. Neither Walt nor anybody else had to say very much. I knew quite well what I was seeing.

After the procedure was over, Walt came into my room and indicated they had spotted a 90–95 percent block in one of the main arteries in my heart.

"Tom, there are three possible courses of action at this point. One would be to take medication, go home, and try to live with the blockage." I could tell from Walt's voice that he had some doubts about that course of action.

"The second alternative would be to undergo angioplasty, where tiny balloons are inserted through a catheter into the blocked area. The balloons are inflated, and this is sometimes successful in removing the blockage. Since the blockage is near the juncture of one artery to another, two balloons would be required, and this would be a very difficult procedure to perform successfully." I could tell that Walt didn't feel this was the best alternative either.

Finally, Walt said, "The third thing we could do is bypass. We would take some veins from another part of your body and bypass the partially blocked artery. I think this would allow you to return to a completely active life."

It didn't take long to make the choice, and I told him that I wanted to go ahead and have the bypass.

I overheard Nancy explain to others later, "Tom's a percentage man. He's always quoting percentages in football, and the percentage favored surgery over the other alternatives."

A short time later Dr. Deepak Gangahar came in and informed me he would be the surgeon in charge of the operation. I was really impressed with his professionalism and his manner. He told me that 1.5 percent of the individuals undergoing open heart surgery of the type I was going to have don't make it. Obviously the odds were very good, and yet 1.5 percent is still larger than you would like when your life is at stake.

Dr. Steve Carveth, a friend of mine from Fellowship of Christian Athletes activities, stopped by and indicated he would be assisting in the operation. I really appreciated this, as I felt that the doctors involved were very professional and competent.

That evening my whole family was with me in the hospital, and we had a good time visiting with Woody Varner, the president of the University of Nebraska Foundation and former president of the University of Nebraska. Woody had been president of the university when I was named head coach and has always been with me at the tough times, always after tough losses, and he was with me now. Woody had recently had bypass surgery and talked about his experiences. He always makes me smile, and this night was no exception. We all enjoyed each other's company. At the end of the evening we had a family prayer about the situation.

After everyone had left, I was a little restless for half an hour or so. Eventually I was able to lift the whole matter up in prayer and surrender it into God's hands. I felt considerable peace and slept soundly that night.

The next morning the nurses woke me at 6:30. I was ready to go, anxious to get on with the thing.

Surgery was uneventful. A double bypass was required because the blockage was near the joining of two arteries, but the surgeons were able to use veins from my chest to do the bypass rather than veins from my legs. This was a plus for my recovery, but caused the procedure to take longer. The whole operation lasted a little over three hours.

I recall little of the rest of the day. I was in a haze because of medication. I spent that time in intensive care with lots of tubes coming out of my body. I'm sure my family visited, and I was able to talk to them, but I remember very little of what actually happened.

Over the next five days, however, I was feeling well enough that I was able to reflect a good deal on my situation. One of the things most noticeable was that my whole self-image had been changed drastically by the open heart surgery. I had always considered myself to be physically indestructible. In twenty-three years of coaching I had never missed a day of practice or coaching due to illness. I had been able to drive myself very hard and had been fortunate to avoid any type of serious illness. But now, all of a sudden, I had broken down.

Obviously my lifestyle may have had something to do with this. The question now was, "What do I do with the time I have left?" I had been very fortunate to have been spared a serious, and possibly fatal, heart attack considering the condition the artery was in. But for what purpose?

The big question in my mind was, "How can I best serve God in the time I have remaining?"

After thinking it through carefully (and I had lots of time to do so), I concluded that, at least for now, the best way I could be of service was to continue coaching. As time went on, I felt more and more comfortable with that decision.

Now I recall less about the operation and more about the idiosyncrasies of health care in our land. The first is the matter of "the enema."

The night before surgery a nurse came in my room about 9:00 and announced, "Mr. Osborne, you have to have an enema." This was something I hadn't had since I was three or four years old.

"You've got the wrong guy. My problem is with my heart, not my...er...my stomach." When I could see that manuever wasn't working, I began to stall by telling her all kinds of things I had to do. I even toyed with the idea of telling her that coaches don't take enemas, but I could tell from the look in her eye that it didn't make much difference what I said. And, needless to say, the nurse eventually won out.

I used to think doctors ran hospitals, but my stay in the hospital has led me to understand that isn't really true. Nurses run hospitals.

After the operation, I encountered the dreaded "breathing machine." Every two hours a technician would come by with that little monster. I was to exhale into it as hard as I could ten times. Each time the machine was brought by a different operator who would explain in great detail the whole procedure all over to me, and I thought I had had it down pretty well the first time. There were ten little lights on the machine, and if I exhaled hard enough I could light up all ten. The nurses would cheerlead and encourage me to light up eight or nine. I must confess, however, that a few times at 4:00 A.M., five or six lights looked awfully good to me and I couldn't have cared less about lighting up eight or nine.

After I blew into the machine ten times, the technician would glee-fully command me to cough hard four times. This was really excruci-ating. My sternum had been split open and wired together!

Then Walt Weaver informed me that he was going to put me on something called the Pritikin Diet. It's named after Nathan Pritikin, who did considerable research testing thousands of people over sev-eral years and concocted his diet by finding what things people abso-lutely could not stand to eat. He put those in the diet. Anything people universally *liked* to eat he omitted.

A couple of weeks after my surgery, Dr. Pritikin died from leuke-mia, and an autopsy revealed the sixty-nine-year-old had very little thickening of the arteries at death in spite of being diagnosed in the late 1950s as suffering from heart disease. Apparently, his low-fat diet (based on daily exercise and consumption of fruits, vegetables, whole grains, and low amounts of dairy products and other fatty foods) had served him well.

The final blow came when Walt told me that Nancy was going to have to drive me everywhere I went for the next three weeks. This meant she had complete control over me. I would have to wait until she had her makeup on, had to take the route that she wanted to drive, couldn't leave until she was ready, and had to stop what I was doing when she wanted to go. You talk about a stressful situation! That was more than I could handle with a healthy heart!

So I was able to find a little humor in the situation, and apparently so were some other people. As the master of ceremonies at an Omaha Press Club Dinner said shortly after the surgery, "Isn't that just like Tom Osborne. They sent him into the hospital for single-by-pass surgery and he decides to go for two."

All in all, surgery is like losing a football game or having a severe athletic injury. It's not the operation that's important. The critical thing is how you react to it. I hope my response will be positive.

I'm sure the years that I have left will be more meaningful and will be thought out better. Perhaps I will slow down and eat more carefully, and this will be helpful not only to me but to my whole family as well.

The same day as my surgery, a running back from the Kansas City Chiefs named Theotis Brown suffered a heart attack. He spent fourteen days in a hospital intensive care unit. When he emerged, he was a man with a message.

"There are so many clichés you can say about life," he said. "Those that are young feel that life goes on forever. Tasks are often put off until tomorrow. We feel any emotion not expressed can be expressed tomorrow. This life-threatening experience has brought me face-to-face with several fundamental truths. Even with the best efforts of medical and science technology, even with the healthiest lifestyles, even with the most beautiful material resources, tomorrow might never arrive. So, ladies and gentlemen, it is time *today* to ease the burden of those less fortunate. It is time *today* to explore the excitement life has to offer. It is time *today* to tell people that you love them."

I've been given a chance to do these things.

Chapter Sixteen

More Than One Person

Each fall Nancy displays a needlepoint in our kitchen that says: "This marriage has been interrupted to bring you football season."

I met Nancy on a blind date arranged by a friend of mine, Don Fricke, who is a former Nebraska football player and now a successful Lincoln dentist and member of the university's Board of Regents. Actually, he was the one who took Nancy out. I took another girl with me on the double date. Nancy indicated later she didn't think much of me. In fact, she thought I was sort of obnoxious. Maybe that was the reason I had such a hard time getting a date with her. I had thought it was because Nancy was so active on campus, when actually she was suspicious of me because I was an ex-pro football player. She had heard such people weren't to be trusted. But eventually we began to see each other, and after we had been going together only two or three months, I asked her to marry me. She had signed a teaching contract with a California school district and at first wanted to go out there and teach for a year.

"I've tried one long-distance romance," I told her, "and don't want another." Previous "romances" for me had ended with the realization that differences between myself and the woman made any permanent relationship unworkable. But I saw immediately in Nancy a person of similar background and values that made possible a strong, lasting marriage. I was from Hastings and she was from Holdrege, which were very similar towns. My dad managed an auto agency, and hers managed a store. We were both Christians. She had her head on straight and demonstrated balance and a lot of common sense from our first meeting.

I've always made decisions rapidly, and I had reached the point where I knew what I wanted. I was ready. I was twenty-five years old, had lived on both coasts, dated a lot, and been engaged once. I knew what I was looking for. And I was also lonely. It just didn't take long for us to realize the match was right.

So we were married that summer, on August 4, 1962. We had known each other only six or seven months. Over the years, I've found that Nancy's personality complements mine well. I'm very hard-driving and goal oriented, whereas she's more relaxed and less competitive. She has a wonderful sense of humor and has provided good diversions for my intensity.

Nancy graduated that same spring we met and then spent the summer out in Holdrege, Nebraska (about fifty miles west of Hastings), with her parents, getting ready for the wedding. I continued in graduate school at the university, working on my master's degree. After we were married in August, we moved into an apartment in Lincoln and she began to teach school, a position she held for three years. In the meantime I finished my master's and my doctorate in educational psychology.

My doctoral studies went smoothly. But I had to pass a reading examination in Spanish, a language I had taken for just one semester, and also an examination in French, which I had to learn from scratch. Other than those exams, everything involved in my doctoral studies (including a dissertation on test anxiety!) went according to schedule.

My master's degree was something else. The course work was no problem, but I was to write a master's thesis worth six hours credit on programmed learning. I taught football plays to freshman players using teaching machines. The research went well, but my faculty advisor was a real stickler and put me through an ordeal. My thesis was a long one, and I rewrote it almost entirely three times. During the third time, murder was on my mind.

I spent months writing and editing and writing, and I almost came unglued. Later I was able to appreciate the fact that my advisor really wanted me to learn to do good research and to write well, and eventually we became good friends. But it was touch and go for a while.

This experience in graduate school enabled me to learn more about myself. I learned the personality that had worked well in athletic competition was not going to do so well now that my days of physical competition were over.

I had learned when I was younger not to express or examine my feelings—particularly feelings of hostility and anger. I tended to "button up" and suppress angry feelings. Athletics served me well in that I could vent these feelings by playing hard and being aggressive in a way that was socially acceptable. But now that my playing days were over, suppressed feelings of anger emerged. I was mad about having to rewrite the thesis and was overworked in general, trying to coach, teach, and do graduate work. I had no outlet in athletic competition.

I became depressed, was at times unexplainably anxious, and was generally not in good emotional shape. I had to learn to communicate better with Nancy and people I worked with and to let them know how I felt. I even had to learn to take time to *realize* how I felt, as I had gotten very good at ignoring or suppressing emotions and sometimes wasn't even aware of them.

Being a Christian actually made this process more difficult, as I had assimilated the idea that Christians shouldn't hate other people, and somewhat unconsciously I got to the point where I didn't even want to *admit* angry or hostile feelings, much less express them. I gradually came to understand that there is nothing wrong with feeling or being angry and that anger could be handled in ways other than punching somebody out. It could be discussed, it could be expressed verbally, it could be jogged off, and to experience it was not un-Christian.

During those years of graduate school I not only learned things in the classroom, but I also learned how to be a husband, a father, and a friend. I also discovered how to adjust to no longer being an athlete. I have noticed that athletes, particularly those who play professionally, often have adjustment problems when they leave athletics and adapt to a "normal" lifestyle. This was certainly true in my case.

Those were very busy years because I was taking a full graduate load plus teaching four sections of undergraduate educational psychology, or twelve hours, and was also coaching. And of course coaching is not a job where you can punch a time clock. I put a lot of long hours into coaching. Every night I was working late, and every morning I got up early.

Our first child, Mike, was born in 1965, and it was about this time that I started to recruit. Annie was born three years later, and then Suzi was born in December of 1969. Suzi was born with a congenital hip problem that necessitated her having surgery and being in a body cast for six months on two occasions. As you can imagine, she required a great deal of care at those times.

So Nancy was left with three very small children—one not very well—and I was out running around the country recruiting. At the time recruiting didn't end in February. We had no national signing date, so once you got a player committed, you had to keep going back to see him to make sure he hadn't changed his mind. After the season ended in November, I was on the road continually through the end of May.

I was so busy that I didn't realize how difficult a time this was for Nancy. I don't think she had any idea when she married me that she was going to be getting into this kind of situation. She told me later that she was about at her wits' end. It wasn't a case where she was thinking about leaving me, but I think she just didn't know how to cope.

She got involved in the Ecumenical Institute, a religious organization in which she took some courses. She learned that one must accept responsibility for his or her own life. It helped her get a grasp on things spiritually, helped her to deal with her situation in such a way that she was able to continue.

I wasn't completely aware of all the things going on in her life at that time, and while we communicated, maybe we didn't do so as well as we should have. I don't think she was quite as honest as she could have been with me about how tough a time she was having. I thought things were going fine with her.

So Nancy is solid as a rock now, and she's been a good buffer for me in coping with the stress of coaching. She is more removed from coaching than I am, and she has been able to maintain good stability and balance about it. I think she has felt all along that if things didn't work out in coaching, there were other things I could do and there were probably other lifestyles that would be even happier for our family.

So if I were to fail as a coach, I don't think it would really upset her as much as many people think it might. She hasn't hung her life on winning or losing football games, and it's been she who, at the times when I've been discouraged, has been able to share a note of optimism and look at things more objectively.

Nancy is my best friend. I have a lot of people who are good friends, but they're more distant friends. The job I'm in and the type of person I am combine to make me a semi-loner. The position of head football coach isolates a person, and the time demanded by the job is such that any time I have left I want to devote to my family. Therefore I'm not a joiner. I'm not a socialite. I don't usually enjoy going to dinners, parties, and other social occasions. Because I'm required to go to so many things where I'm the speaker or "special guest," when I do finally have some time of my own, I want to spend it with my family. My social life as a result is almost nonexistent.

And we get a lot of strange letters. Some are critical. Some are even made public in the papers. Occasionally I get plays sent to me—trick plays. Often I'll read the letter with a play diagram in it and discover there will be twelve or thirteen men on the field.

One man wrote me letter after letter with a whole new offensive scheme. He obviously spent hours drawing diagrams, and yet most of what he drew was illegal. It wouldn't have the required men on the line of scrimmage, people were in motion toward the line of scrimmage, and so on. Nevertheless, he was very persistent in asking me to use some of these plays. I get a lot of help like that.

On occasion we get some truly nasty letters. I know it affects Nancy when we get them. It's hard for us to understand why people would be vindictive, but some are. The unsigned mail generally goes in the wastebasket, but it's not always forgotten when the garbage gets carried out.

As the children were growing up and the demands on my time to recruit and speak and so on increased, I began to feel the need to be more than one person. I needed to spend time with my children, and we played basketball together in the driveway and tried to play some softball. I played catch with Mike with the football. I tried to go to all their Little League games, basketball games, and so on—all the games I could attend. During the summer, we tried to make up for the time lost during football season and recruiting by spending a week or two at Lake McConaughy in western Nebraska. Lately we have gone skiing as a family in Colorado for four or five days during spring break.

Yet many times I've felt guilty as I went off to speak at banquets two or three nights a week. I've thought about these as times when I could be at home, because I don't *have* to accept those speaking engagements. Yet, professionally, people expect you to show up at certain things. It's very awkward to tell people you cannot or will not attend and speak, but I've gotten better at turning things down in recent years.

I've needed to be a father who spends lots of time with his children. I've needed to be a coach who spends seventy or eighty hours a week coaching. And then I've needed to be a person with enough charisma and enough energy to go out and do a lot of public relations work— speak five, six, seven times a week, if necessary, be on television—all these kinds of things. And so it just sometimes seems there isn't enough time in the day. No person can do all that is expected.

I suppose it says something significant about me—about my priorities and the importance I give to coaching in contrast to being a parent—to say that the most difficult time I've had since becoming head coach had nothing to do with a particular team, player, game, or season. Instead, it related to my son's senior year in high school football.

Through his junior high school years and his sophomore and junior years in high school, Mike had been out for athletics but with only moderate success. He played on the reserve team. He made the varsity basketball team as a junior and played some. He'd always been good enough to be on the team but seldom good enough to play a lot. Finally in his senior season he was named starting quarterback on a reasonably good football team, a team with a pretty strong tradition. He was elected one of the co-captains.

I was concerned because I felt he had ability but little playing time. Experience in quarterbacking is very important.

Mike's first game was against Grand Island, a team that later lost only one or two games that year. Mike played tentatively in the first half, but in the second half I could see he was gaining confidence and a feel for the game. He was poised and playing well, and he took the team on a long drive to score in the last two minutes. With the extra point, the score was tied 14-14.

The game went into overtime, which is now commonly a part of high school football but not in the Division I college game. Grand Island won the toss and made Mike's team try first to score within four plays from the ten yard line. Mike completed a short pass on first down. On the next play he got an early snap from center and dropped the ball. He picked it up and took off for the end zone. He made it about five yards when he was hit from the side just short of the goal line. I don't think he saw the guy coming, and he fumbled the ball into the end zone. A player from his team and a player from the opposing team dove for the ball, but the opposing player got it. Then all Grand Island really had to do with its series of downs from the ten yard line was run one play and kick a field goal to win the game 17-14.

The next week Mike's team played Omaha Westside, a team that eventually became state champion. Nobody even came close to them except Mike's team. Westside was undefeated for two straight years, probably one of the best high school squads ever to play in Nebraska. "We" trailed 7-6 on a missed point-after-touchdown early in the game, and I thought Mike was playing fairly well. Suddenly, there was a tremendous deluge, three or four inches of rain. The officials stopped the game for an hour and finally resumed play in a light rain. Heavy rain returned occasionally, and the field became a quagmire. The game ended 7-6. Under the circumstances, Mike's team played a tremendous game against a very strong squad with four or five players who went on to major colleges.

I realized Mike's team was now 0-2, and things get a little tight when you're quarterback and your team is winless and hasn't scored many points. The next game against Lincoln Southeast was again played on a very muddy field with a wet football. "We" scored a touchdown early, again failed on the point-after, and the other team answered quickly. Mike's team went down the field again before being slowed. They had four shots from the one yard line but didn't get in. As the game went on the 7-6 score held, the ball got wetter and the field got muddier, and I could see Mike's confidence sliding. He was intercepted a couple of times and had a couple of fumbles from the wet ball.

I knew after the game that there was good chance he would be replaced. I felt very bad. I knew he had come close to getting the job done. But he was benched, and he really never got much opportunity to play after that. I felt it was hard on him particularly because he was my son. When your dad is a coach, it's sometimes assumed you ought to be especially knowledgeable or talented. Of course that's not always true.

That was 1983. My own team went 12-1 that fall and played very well, but I think I sometimes felt worse over Mike's situation than I enjoyed my own. It was very hard to stand by and watch. I could understand that the coach did what he thought he had to, and yet I felt bad because I knew Mike had always been on the threshold of accomplishing some fine things in athletics.

It was a difficult experience, and yet I suppose that, as with all experiences, I learned from it. It sharpened my awareness of how parents of my players feel when their sons don't make the progress they hope for. It served me well from that standpoint. In the long run, it might have been a maturing time for Mike, too. I'm sure he grew up more that football season than he would have if everything had gone smoothly. It just illustrates the fact that life isn't always fair.

Athletics is a hard task-master, and some of the key factors aren't really in our hands, things such as missed PAT's, officiating, and injuries. Yet that's the way life is. It's not always the way you want it.

The critical thing, however, isn't the adversity. The important factor is how we *react* to adversity. I see a lot of pain in athletics. The saving grace of it all, as far as I'm concerned, is the knowledge that out of pain and adversity so often we develop strength, and our true character becomes evident.

Chapter Seventeen

A Crash Course in Flying

The Wright brothers' father is supposed to have said, "If man were meant to fly he'd have wings." I got into flying out of self-defense.

Actually I had no great attraction to flying, but I spent a lot of time in private planes recruiting, going to speaking engagements, one thing or another. Many times the pilot I was flying with was somebody I'd never seen before. Sometimes before a speaking engagement people would send a plane and a pilot to get me and I would have no idea what kind of plane it would be or what kind of experience the pilot had.

One time I flew to Wichita in unbelievably bad weather to speak at a banquet. We encountered rain, sleet, hail, and turbulance. I was sure the pilot was in over his head, but we made it.

Sometimes I would get in with pilots who were really old, and the thought crossed my mind, *If something happened to this guy, I'm pretty well done. There is nothing I can do*! So I thought it would be a good idea to learn how to fly. If something did happen to the pilot, I could at least get the plane down on the ground and live to tell about it.

Like many of the things I've had to do, learning to fly was kind of a crash course—that's a bad term—kind of a quick course. I had to start lessons when spring practice was over and get it finished before we started practicing in the fall. And that's what I did.

I finished in late July and got a private license. I accumulated a total of maybe forty-five hours of flight time in the process. Then I didn't fly in September, October, or November because of the football season, and did very little flying in December, January, or February.

Our family decided to go skiing in March. By then I had a total of sixty hours and was checked out in a larger airplane that would carry six people, a Piper single-engine plane. So we loaded the plane heavily with all of our warm clothes, ski equipment, and a full tank of gas and headed down the runway on the start of our trip to Denver. The only problem was that all the experience I had flying was with two passengers, no luggage, and a light load of fuel. When I hit normal lift-off speed—around seventy-five knots—I lifted the nose of the airplane and we got off the ground all of three or four feet before the plane slammed back down onto the runway with a thump. We were a little out of balance, and the plane swerved when we hit the runway. It wasn't particularly dangerous, but it frightened my family badly.

I got the plane stopped and my family caught its breath. I went to another runway directed a little more into the wind and got the speed built up a bit more, and we took off for Denver. Not too wisely I decided to go into Denver's Stapleton International Airport. There's a lot of heavy traffic there. The tower had me headed into one of the larger runways. Everything was going smoothly.

Then, a half-mile off the runway, the air traffic controller told me to divert to a runway parallel to the one I was approaching but a couple hundred yards to the side of it. So I banked hard into some stiff crosswinds. Everyone slammed to one side of the plane as it swerved over. And for the second time on this family flying trip we slammed into a runway. When my family got out of the airplane, they were well convinced that this was not a very good way to travel.

All the way home a week later Mike was ill. "Motion sickness," I said.

"Panic!" Nancy and the kids contended.

Not long after that, we took off on another trip and the door on the airplane wasn't completely closed. As we got in the air and built up speed, the wind coming through the partially opened door was making a lot of noise. Nancy, assuming the plane was pressurized, thought somebody was going to get sucked out into the sky. So she grabbed hold of Mike, sitting closest to the door, and screamed for me to put the plane on the ground. It was bedlam. Suzi was praying in the back seat, Annie was crying—I couldn't take the commotion, so I landed and closed the door.

Two or three months after that, on the way to a vacation, we landed at a small airport in central Nebraska to avoid a thunderstorm. I came in a little fast and had trouble slowing the plane on the short runway. We used up the whole runway and then ran off about a hundred yards onto the grass, stopping within view of a fence. Again, this proved to be a disconcerting experience to my family, and it's about the last time the whole family has been willing to do much flying with me. In fact, most of my flying is a solo experience now.

Fishing is my favorite pastime, and more than anything else I would like to have my family like to fish too. But I've been somewhat self-defeating.

When my kids were little, many times we'd be out in the boat for four or five hours at a stretch, and of course they didn't really enjoy it at their young ages. That started some negative feelings toward fishing. By the time Mike was six or seven years old, he'd caught a wall-eye that weighed 11 pounds, a striped bass that weighed 14 or 15 pounds, and a 6- or 7-pound rainbow trout. He had many of the greater thrills a fisherman could have.

So I think the combination of my overdoing it, and the fact that he had done a lot at an early age, led to the fact that he really doesn't care much about fishing. My daughters are somewhat the same way, and my wife is too. So it's like my flying. It's one of my big passions, and something I end up doing mostly by myself.

Chapter Eighteen

National Championships and Other Vagaries

Penn State's Joe Paterno and I were talking about the national championship after our 1984 Orange Bowl loss to Miami when he said, "You know, some year you're gonna win it when you really don't think you've got a chance."

He reminded me about that statement later that year during a telephone conversation the week before we played Oklahoma in the fall. We were ranked number one in the nation at the time. "This could be the year," he said. "After losing all those great players, it didn't appear as though you'd have a chance." Then we lost to Oklahoma and the "chance" was gone again.

But the national championship has not really been as big an obsession with me as people might think. My objective is, and has always been, to put a good football team on the field every week, prepare well, play hard, and then just take our rewards as they come and our lumps if they don't. We really can't very well set the national championship as our goal because it depends so much on factors beyond our control such as schedule, injuries, and the ballot box.

In 1982 we lost to Penn State 27-24 in the fourth game of the season on a controversial touchdown with four seconds left. Two weeks later they were beaten by Alabama by twenty-one points and dropped well down in the ratings. Three or four weeks later we were playing Iowa State and were ranked second or third in the country, ahead of Penn State who was playing Notre Dame. Then Joe Paterno made a comment picked up by the national media to the effect that if Penn State beat Notre Dame, they would deserve consideration for the top spot. They beat Notre Dame, whose starting quarterback was sidelined with an injury, by a couple of touchdowns. We beat Iowa State by thirty-eight points. At that point Iowa State might have been about as good a football team as Notre Dame, but it didn't have the national image. And yet I knew Joe's statement would be read by lots of people and that their win over Notre Dame would be more influential than our win over Iowa State. And, sure enough, they moved ahead of us in the national rankings.

They won the rest of their games and we won the rest of ours, and they stayed ahead of us in the rankings. Our only loss was by three points in a controversial game at Penn State, while their loss was by twenty-one points to Alabama (not a highly ranked team that year). They lost after we lost, and normally the procedure in national championship balloting is that whoever loses last gets penalized. We finished 12-1, they were 11-1. But Penn State was named national champion.

I'm not quarreling that Penn State didn't deserve to be national champion. After all, they beat us and they beat Georgia in the Sugar Bowl. The point is the vote could have gone either way, or for Southern Methodist University, which was undefeated but tied once that year. The schedule and the vote determined the national championship, not the teams.

Another interesting national championship race was the 1983 season, which culminated in the Orange Bowl of 1984. We wound up 12-1, losing to Miami in a very close game on Miami's home field by one point when we probably could have tied the game by kicking an extra point. Miami was 11-1 but had been beaten badly by Florida early in the season. Most people who follow football concede that Nebraska was the most dominant team of 1983, but our loss came in the last game and Miami's came early, and Miami finished number one. Remember, the year before just the opposite occurred. Our loss to Penn State came early and theirs came later, but they finished on top.

This just points up the fact that what we're voting on is not clearly stated. Do we vote for who we think is the best team, or do we vote for the best record? Does *when* you lose matter? I don't know the answer to these questions. I vote in the United Press International poll (voted for Penn State in 1983 and Miami in 1984, incidentally, since they beat us head-to-head), yet I have never seen a list of voting criteria. In short, I'm as confused as anyone.

Obviously a national playoff is desirable. However, there are more than one hundred teams in Division I football. In order to have a meaningful elimination (as in basketball), you would need to have a fairly lengthy playoff and abolish the bowls as they now exist. Nobody seems to want to change the bowls, so then you start getting into a playoff after the bowls, and this runs into the USFL draft, second semester, the Hula Bowl, East-West Game, Senior Bowl, and so on. Nobody seems to be able to present a plan that enough people can support. And one hundred major college teams competing for only one championship spot means there would be an awful lot of losers, far more than there are after the bowl season is finished.

Many people question how Brigham Young University could ever be voted the nation's number one team of 1984-85. "Their schedule was too weak. Never played a top-twenty team." Arguments like that.

I voted for BYU. What they did was beat every team on their schedule, which no other school in our division could claim. They did everything expected of them, everything they could do with the schedule they had.

They never tripped up, the way we did at Syracuse, Oklahoma did at Kansas, and other teams did along the way. And they got as much out of their talent as there was to get.

They deserved the national championship—at least under our present system and at least as much as some others who have received the title in the past. By the way, I've never voted Nebraska to the top spot at the end of a season. Sometimes *during* the year I've voted us number one, but never at the end. The most tempted I've been to change that was after the 1984 Orange Bowl loss to Miami, because we were so much stronger at the end of the game. But still, it was a loss in a game that we knew was for the national championship.

The writers voted us the team most likely to win the Big Eight Conference title in 1984, which shocked me because of the heavy graduation losses we had from the great 1983 team. We lost eight starters from the offense including the top two quarterbacks, and anytime you're replacing a starting quarterback, you have to be concerned. We had just three offensive starters returning, none of them at the skill positions. We had eight or nine defensive starters returning, but our defense had ranked about seventieth in the nation the year before.

So we had several questions to answer and could see ourselves very easily going .500 in 1984. I thought we'd be good enough to probably beat Wyoming and Minnesota. I thought the UCLA game would be a tossup. Even though we'd beaten them badly the year before, I thought the Syracuse game would be difficult. They had a lot of people back who had played well at the end of 1983 (when they beat West Virginia and Boston College). And their Carrier Dome is a very tough place to play. Then we would start the Big Eight Conference schedule with Oklahoma State and Missouri, who both had a lot of returning starters from good teams. So we had four games right there that I thought would either make us or break us. I thought we could easily end up losing two or three of those four games.

As it turned out we lost only to Syracuse, and I think part of it was that Syracuse had been concentrating on that game for a year. They worked hard on it. They were at an emotional peak. The place they play in is very noisy. And then we had an injury problem. Our starting fullback, Tom Rathman, was knocked out on the opening kickoff, and Craig Sundberg, our quarterback, was playing sub-par with a bad shoulder. He hadn't thrown the ball all week. Jeff Smith, our starting I-back, didn't play because of a sprained ankle, and our second I-back, Paul Miles, lasted just two plays before dislocating a shoulder.

They whipped us. They deserved to win the game. And when we

responded well and won those first two games in the Big Eight sched-ule and then beat Colorado who, like Syracuse, had pointed for us all year, I felt we had a solid team. And we kept on winning until Okla-homa. In many respects, we played well enough to win that game too.

I was talking to Saints' head coach Bum Phillips in New Orleans fol-lowing our loss to Oklahoma and before the 1985 Sugar Bowl. He said, "You know, I've been in this game a long time, and there are some times when you just don't win. You've done everything that you need to do to win, but you just don't win."

I think that's something a lot of people don't understand. There are random factors involved. When somebody wins, the assumption is they're just better and if you played them ten times they would win ten times. That isn't the way it is. There's a chance factor.

In that Oklahoma game, for instance, we missed three field goals. One of them was far enough away that we probably had a 30–50 per-cent chance of making it. One of them was medium range and we probably would have made 60–70 percent of those. And one was al-most point blank range where we'd make 90 percent. The odds of missing all three, if you work it out mathematically, may be one-in-thirty or one-in-forty. But we missed all three. It's not likely it would happen that way again.

We also had a tough call go against us. And, most importantly, we failed to score on fourth down with the ball only inches from their goal line late in the game. There was a good deal of unhappiness and sec-ond guessing about that fourth and inches call, as most Nebraska fans saw it as the one cause of our not winning the national championship.

I've taken a lot of heat from time to time for calls or decisions I've made. But we had one situation in the 1982 Orange Bowl (following the 1981 season) that got us a lot more credit than we deserved.

We were playing undefeated and number-one-ranked Clemson and were trailing by fifteen points at the start of the fourth quarter. Early in the period we scored, and of course I felt we needed to go for a two-point conversion because we needed two touchdowns and two two-point conversions to win the game. I took time out to talk to our quarterback, Mark Mauer. I told him to call a play-action pass to the right but if he saw a strong safety blitz coming, he was to audible a pitch play to the left, away from the blitz. Mark went on the field and somehow there was confusion. We got a delay of game penalty. That put us back to the eight yard line. Of course, now I just wanted a pass play from eight yards out. It was too far out for the weak side pitch audible. I was sure Mark would realize that.

As we lined up again, we still had the play-action pass called. Mark saw the strong safety blitz coming. I could see the blitz coming, too, heard the longer cadence, and suddenly realized what Mark was doing. He was changing to the pitch. I was in shock. "No, Mark!" I yelled.

But it was very noisy, and our tight end missed the audible entirely and didn't even block the defensive end. The left guard normally would pull to the left, but he didn't hear the audible either and didn't pull. The left tackle was the only player on that side of the line who seemed to hear the audible, and he blocked the tackle. Fortunately the I-back, Roger Craig, heard the audible and took the pitch and went left. A couple of players from Clemson, normally a great defensive team, reacted poorly. I think they really reacted to the missed blocks. Roger went around the end, side-stepped the cornerback, and made it all the way in. It was unbelievable! We blocked only one person and still scored.

We almost scored again and would have had a chance to tie the game, but we came up short on a fourth down play in the last few minutes of the game. But after the game a number of people congratulated me on what a tremendous call the quick pitch for the two-point conversion was when everyone was expecting a pass. Of course, it was really the *wrong* play, but it was so messed up it worked. I just mumbled, "Thank you," and tried to change the subject.

Yet we've had other situations where we've run plays that were well thought out, that went into the exact point of the defense we wanted to attack, and that for one reason or another came up short. And of course those calls have sometimes been widely condemned because they didn't work. "Good" calls are the ones that work. "Bad" calls are the ones that don't.

Chapter Nineteen

The Nebraska Cycle

While we haven't won a national championship since 1971, Nebraska has had twenty-three consecutive winning seasons, sixteen consecutive years with bowl appearances, and fifteen consecutive years of finishing in the Associated Press or United Press International Top Ten.

The question I'm asked most frequently by the media—and I was never asked it more often than during the 1984 season when we made it twice to the number one ranking after losing so many great stars from the 1983 squad—is "Why is Nebraska so consistently good?"

That's an important question to address. No publisher would have asked me to write this book if Nebraska hadn't been winning a lot of games. And Nebraska wouldn't have been winning a lot of games if it weren't for a lot of factors.

First let me say that athletics is always cyclical. Nobody wins forever, and this will be true of Nebraska. We've been fortunate to have a very long-lasting cycle, however. And it does appear to me there are some special factors, perhaps unique to Nebraska, that may have contributed to the longevity of Nebraska's success.

An obvious factor is the tremendous stability at Nebraska. Our assistant coaches average fourteen years at Nebraska. Cletus Fischer, our offensive line and kickers coach, has been at Nebraska twenty-five years. John Melton, our linebacker coach, twenty-three years. Defensive end coach George Darlington has been with us twelve years, and offensive line coach Milt Tenopir has been with us eleven years. Defensive coordinator Charlie McBride and receiver's coach Gene Huey are eight year veterans at Nebraska.

The stability of our staff has allowed us to have great continuity in our recruiting. Each coach gets to know the high school coaches and athletes well in his assigned geographic area. Any time you have to replace a coach, you generally lose the whole recruiting season in his part of the country. On many coaching staffs, two or three assistants are replaced almost every year, and this is very disruptive.

The continuity of our coaching staff has also been helpful in terms of our knowing what to do on the playing field. We don't have to spend time in meetings coaching the coaches. When I say something about a "scoop" block, our offensive line coaches know what I mean. When we talk about a "cover 9," all our defensive coaches know how that coverage works. We don't have to spend a lot of time explaining terminology to each other.

There's also tremendous loyalty surrounding Nebraska, not just by the coaches, but by the fans as well. Our fans can really focus on Nebraska football because there are no other major colleges and no professional teams in the state, and other recreational pursuits are somewhat limited. At times this focus can be uncomfortable as there is practically no "off-season" for Nebraska football. You can read something about Nebraska football in the major newspapers in the state on almost a daily basis, even in the spring and summer months.

Because Nebraska football is so important to people in the state, it's attractive for young men to play here. Every player likes doing something well in front of people who appreciate his efforts. We've had more than one-hundred-thirty consecutive sellouts in Memorial Stadium, and almost any game we play within five hundred miles of Nebraska will be sold out because our fans will buy up any empty seats in those stadiums. With this type of interest, of course, comes pressure. But I would rather have pressure because people care than apathy because they have no interest.

One positive example of the intense fan support has been our Lincoln Parent Program. Several years ago, one of our assistant coaches suggested we pair up each player who was recruited that year with a Lincoln family who would serve as a support family for the player. The idea was that this would enable him to get out of the dormitory, get away from football for a while, and possibly serve to encourage him in down times, times of discouragement.

I was a little reluctant to accept the idea. I thought there wouldn't be enough families to go around and that many of the players wouldn't like the idea. I thought they would want to be more independent. But to my surprise, the program has met with great enthusiasm on the part of most of our players and a great many families in Lincoln. We actually have a waiting list of families who want to get involved with the players in this way.

We've had to be careful about making sure it is all in compliance with NCAA rules. Each year we have the new group of Lincoln families meet in the summer before their players arrive. We hand out a list of rules, reminding the "parents" they can't lend players money or cars, do the players' laundry, and a whole series of other "don'ts." When the players arrive on campus in the fall, we have a meeting with the Lincoln parents and their players together, and again we review the rules so there is no misunderstanding about what can and cannot be done. We've found this program has helped us retain players because the support of these families has tended to minimize homesickness and other adjustment problems that most athletes experience when they are away from home for the first time.

Another factor that's helpful is the tradition at Nebraska. We've been fortunate to have a string of many years of reasonably good football teams, bowl games, and national television exposure, and this makes it possible for us to go to almost any high school in the country, talk to the top player in that school, and have some degree of acceptance. Most will give us careful consideration.

Our geographical situation in the center of the country is a positive factor, too, for it makes it possible for us to recruit on both coasts and as far south as Texas and Louisiana and up into the Dakotas and Minnesota. Our location is not an unmitigated blessing, however, as we do have cold weather during the recruiting season, and we're not close to any large population center where there are large numbers of outstanding football players. But neither do we receive great recruiting competition from other major football programs in our own state, so we get most of the outstanding high school athletes in the state to attend the University of Nebraska. We're also able to attract a fairly high quality of walk-on player because so many of the players in Nebraska have a strong desire to play at the university.

I also think it's important that we've generally been able to attract players who not only have ability but who also have excellent character and work habits. I've often felt our players have outworked opponents more than they have outshown them with talent. New coaches on our staff have marveled at how hard our players work during the off-season compared to players at other places they've been. We've had players who've had to wait a year or two or even three to play, and they've done this with a good attitude. They also have been self-sacrificing in terms of not caring too much who gets publicity. They've really been enjoyable to coach because of their attitude, their character, and their willingness to work hard.

Still another factor that has been very important to our program has been the supportive attitude of the university administration, Board of Regents, and athletic department officials, especially Bob Devaney. Since Bob was on the sideline so many years, he's quite understanding of the vagaries of football and has done all he could to be supportive and to run interference. I'm sure there have been times when Bob was tempted to interfere or second guess, but he never has, and that's a real testimony to his professional stature.

There's also a developmental quality that may be unique to Nebraska. We try to develop young men more fully than many university football programs. We accept a lot of walk-ons, treat them like all the scholarshiped players, and give them an opportunity to learn and mature in our freshman program and schedule. We also save five to eight scholarships each year to award to the walk-ons who pay the price and develop into promising players. Thirty-five to forty percent of our starters each year began their careers as walk-ons, which I think is a remarkable statistic.

We have the most comprehensive and sophisticated weight training program I know of anywhere to develop young men to their optimum size and strength. Boyd Epley has coordinated that important aspect of our athletic department for fifteen years.

Boyd was a pole-vaulter at Nebraska in the late sixties and got involved in body building and weightlifting. As a result, he began to gain weight and also to break a number of poles as he vaulted. This was hazardous to his well-being and was also rather expensive for the track team, so he started to talk to Bob Devaney about weight training for football players. Bob gradually began to appreciate his ideas and to give him more and more leeway, and over the years Boyd has developed a truly outstanding strength program. He is possibly as knowledgeable a strength coach as there is in the country and a very creative person in the use of computerized weight programs and the development of different types of weight machines. He has done an outstanding job of building players, some of whom have had rather marginal talents, into great athletes. More than sixteen of his former assistants have gone on to be full-time strength coaches for professional and other major college programs.

Football can be aided more by a weight training program than almost any other sport. I don't believe football relies nearly as much on natural ability as do basketball and baseball. Particularly at the line positions, linebackers, defensive ends, and tight ends, players can do a lot to make themselves into great players through a weight training program, which is not just lifting weights, but also focusing on flexibility, agility, and speed. All of these things are incorporated into our off-season program.

One of the more dramatic cases of what this program can do is Mike Tranmer. Mike came to us as a 180-pound walk-on nose guard from Lyons, Nebraska. By working very hard in the weight room, Mike eventually went up to about 240 pounds and improved his speed and strength dramatically. He was bigger, faster, and quicker. He made tremendous progress, played a good deal as a sophomore and junior, and was able to start for us as a senior.

When I took over as head coach in 1973, I realized I would no longer have the time to also serve as the academic counselor. I got a letter about that time from a Catholic nun named Ursula, who told me that she had been observing our study hall and thought it was not particularly well run. Further, she felt she could do a better job. I don't know if she knew I was the academic counselor in charge of that study hall or not. At any rate, with some irritation, I threw the letter in the wastebasket, only to receive another letter two weeks later stating the same case. At that point, partly because of her perseverance and partly because I wanted to talk to the person who had the gall to write letters like this, I invited her to come see me. It didn't take too long for me realize that any person who spoke as persuasively as she, and who had the personal qualities she had, would indeed do a better job of running our academic program than was being done. So Ursula Walsh was hired and has done an outstanding job of working with our athletes.

The first benefit of the academic counseling program is that it helps in recruiting. If parents are fairly well-assured that their young man's academic needs will be looked after satisfactorily, the player is a bit more apt to enroll here. Secondly, I think it's very important for the players to feel they have someone who really cares about their academic progress and also is proficient in trying to discern their needs, fill out their schedules, help with their tutoring, run an adequate study hall, and so on. In this respect, we feel that Ursula and her assistant, Marsha Shada, are two of the very best academic counselors in the country. Ursula has now been here long enough and has been successful enough that she has a good national image. One of the situations that justifiably helped earn her this reputation was that of Junior Miller.

Junior came to us from Midland, Texas. He managed to get out of high school with a diploma but also with a severe reading disorder called dyslexia. By setting up remedial help and some rather sophisticated tutoring programs, Ursula was able to improve Junior's reading to the point where he was not only able to stay in college but also to do reasonably well academically. He played for four years here, then became a successful professional player. I think Ursula did a tremendous job of enhancing Junior's study skills *and* his future.

Ursula is more effective than one might expect because she is a woman and has a bit of a motherly image about her, although she can be very stern at the appropriate time. I think the players relate well to her because of her femininity, but there are times when she will call on me or one of the other coaches to be the "heavy" if a player is not responding as he should. Then we'll enter the picture and get after him.

During Ursula's thirteen years at Nebraska, we've had more than twice the number of Academic All-Big Eight players as any other school in the conference and nearly twice the number of Academic All-Americans as any school in the *country*.

The coaches we've had at Nebraska have been extremely diligent in recruiting and in preparing for games. The normal work week during the football season and recruiting is fourteen hours a day, seven days a week. We average at least forty hours a week during the spring and summer, with three weeks off for vacation. On an hourly basis, coaches are not well paid. The life of an assistant coach involves not only long hours but also little security. If something happens to the head coach, there are few guarantees for the assistants. One really has to enjoy coaching to stay with it in view of all of the drawbacks.

I've tried to give each assistant coach an area of responsibility and then let him do the job, much as Bob Devaney did with me. I've also tried to work right along with the assistant coaches, because I've felt it is important that I put in the same hours and expend the same effort as they do. They are bound to have more dedication toward the job if they feel I'm taking the approach "Do as I do" rather than only "Do as I say."

It must be discouraging at times for the assistant coaches to read or hear of the things that "I" have accomplished in terms of won-lost records, championships, and honors. In reality, all of us know that it truly is "we" who have done those things. Many times I've seen myself as only a small part of whatever success we've had. Each assistant coach, in his own way, makes as great a contribution as I do.

The long cycle of success of Nebraska has taken the effort and dedication of all of us. Nebraska has been blessed with some great assistant coaches, and with great coaches' wives, too. A head coach can be no more effective than his assistants, and his assistants can be no more effective than their wives will let them be.

Remember Nancy's needlepoint in our kitchen? It's a fact of the coaching life.

Chapter Twenty

More Than Winning

Pepper Rodgers and I once shared a cab on the way from the airport to a coaches' convention in San Francisco. During the conversation, Pepper commented, "There are only two kinds of coaches—those who have been fired and those who are going to get fired."

Pepper's statement startled me. At that time I was a fairly new head coach, and I wondered about the accuracy of his statement. As the years have gone by, I've observed that what he was saying had a good deal of truth in it.

When I arrived at the convention hotel, I looked around the opulent lobby and the stuffy meeting rooms, and I noticed there weren't many coaches who were in their fifties, and virtually none who were in their sixties. Contrast this to a convention of attorneys, doctors, or other professions where people often remain active into their sixties and even seventies. Between 1972 and 1984, there were eighteen head football coaching changes in the Big Eight Conference, an average of more than two coaching changes per school during those twelve years. Coaching is definitely a high risk profession.

Over the years I've come to realize that a large percentage of the people who leave coaching do so not just because they are fired but also because the coaches have put too much pressure on *themselves*.

Coaches drive *themselves* out of the game. *Coaches*—not the administration, alumni, or media—have been unable to handle failure because they've had a wrong definition of success and an inappropriate philosophy of the game.

I've gotten away from measuring success in terms of wins and losses. It's a mistake those of us in coaching too often make when we define a good season as winning a certain number of games or a championship. It's very difficult year-in and year-out to win the number of games that the fans, the press, the alumni, or even the coaches themselves feel is necessary to be successful.

Therefore, it's made sense to me to measure success more in terms of how closely a team has come to realizing its potential. As a result, I've almost never talked to a team about setting a goal of winning a particular football game but of getting into *position* to win the game. The important thing is to play the best we are able to play. If we do that, we should be able to live with the consequences.

We set a variety of goals each week, usually on Tuesday for a Saturday game. For instance, on offense we'll try to determine the number of yards we think we ought to be able to attain rushing, the number of yards we would like to have passing, the number of points we think we can score, the number of turnovers we want to limit ourselves to, and the number of penalties we think we can live with. Then defensively, we set some objectives to limit our opponents to a certain number of yards rushing and passing, a certain number of points, turnovers, penalty yards, and so on. We also have objectives in the kicking game such as average yards gained on kickoffs and punt returns, and yards yielded to our opponent's returns.

We break the game down in this way, trying to meet those objectives. And if we meet enough of them—play well enough, give enough effort—we feel we'll be in position to win the game. But if we're able to meet most of these objectives and still lose, we feel in many ways we're still successful. We've come close to playing as well as we can.

Success, as far as I'm concerned, cannot be measured in terms of wins. It's more than winning. It's how close we're coming to playing as well as we can. By this measure it's possible for more people to feel good about themselves as athletes and coaches. They can see a realistic standard and some progress. Then they're not going to be driven out of the profession by their own or others' negative feelings about their performance.

I don't mean to diminish the tremendous stress in coaching or demean the coaches who leave the profession for health reasons, emotional burn-out, feelings of failure, and the fatigue of putting up with constant criticism. But a well-thought-out philosophy of coaching in most cases is essential to being able to stay in the profession for any length of time.

My personal philosophy of coaching is this: "To make an effort to win in a manner that reflects well on the university, that promotes the personal development of the players, and that has a positive effect on young people."

A president of a major university said somewhat facetiously a number of years ago, "I'm hoping to build a university that the football team could be proud of." Unfortunately, there are some in our society who would have athletics be the tail that wags the dog. I don't believe this is healthy.

Football should blend in with the academic process. It's important that university and faculty administration feel the football program fits into the overall mission of the institution, and I think this general feeling prevails at the University of Nebraska. As I mentioned earlier, we've had more Academic All-American players in the last ten years than any other school in the country (by almost a 2-1 margin), more than double the number of Academic All-Big Eight players of any other school in our conference during the same period, and an 85–90 percent graduation rate of those who have completed their eligibility over the last ten years. These are academic accomplishments that are in keeping with what the university feels is appropriate.

Another aspect of reflecting well on the institution is operating within National Collegiate Athletic Association rules, and I am very proud of the fact that our program has not been in serious difficulty with the NCAA and has not undergone a major NCAA investigation during the past twenty-three years. I think most people we recruit against and compete with believe we operate within the rules. This certainly means as much to me as having a desirable win-loss record.

Promoting the personal development of players is a bit more complex than promoting the image of the school. Even though players may be very large physically, they still often have fragile psyches. At times, athletics can be destructive to their sense of self-worth and personal development. Therefore, it's important that we coaches do what we can to give our players the feeling that we accept them and like them as people first and players second. Some of them will have to be third- and fourth-stringers, some of them will be disappointed in their playing time, and some of them will be injured. As we alter their position on the depth chart and as we attempt to mold them into better players by disciplining them, it is very important that we continue to reinforce the idea that they have personal worth. We try to do this by being as positive with them as we can genuinely be. It's important to spend as much time talking about the things a player does well as we spend describing what he needs to improve.

I try to visit with each player in a personal interview in my office at least once a year and spend as much time off the field as I can in talking with them individually. Each position coach meets with his players on at least two or three occasions each year as he reviews their academic and football progress. And of course our academic counselor spends a lot of time in discussing their personal affairs as well as their academic progress.

The "old" way of dealing with players often had overtones of a boot camp mentality where players were treated as objects and were disciplined in dehumanizing ways. This can be effective in developing a football team, but it also has left some psychological scars on players that have been a long time healing and so is not worth what it costs even when it is "successful."

Another aspect of personal development that I think is very important is the matter of *discipline*. In our society today there are many young people who encounter very little tangible and consistent discipline in their lives, and athletics has been able to provide a beneficial discipline structure for many players. The simple disciplines of having to come to practice at a certain time every day, having to do certain things in the weight room in the off-season, and making a certain kind of consistent effort on the practice field enable a player to begin to gain some control over his life and enable him to become more disciplined in other endeavors. A good example of what hard work and discipline can accomplish is the story of Andy Means.

Andy came to us as a freshman walk-on who weighed 160 pounds and ran a 4.9 forty-yard dash. He had played defensive end in high school and told us he wanted to be a defensive back. He had a lot to learn and didn't have great physical ability, so he played on the lowest freshman defensive unit. But he worked very hard in the weight room. He red-shirted, got his weight to over 180 pounds and his forty-yard time to under 4.5 seconds, and eventually played for us as a three-year starter at cornerback. His discipline led to a remarkable transformation. We have had countless cases like Andy's over the years, and this is one of the truly gratifying aspects of coaching.

Another factor involved in personal development is learning to make the *effort* to be the *best* a person can be. This type of effort brings a person up against the limits of his capability, and this, in turn, promotes self-knowledge. A player begins to understand more about himself as he is taxed to the limit and isn't sure how he'll measure up. Such was the case of Brian Hiemer.

Brian came to us in 1980 as a 180-pound walk-on from David City, Nebraska. He was cut in the spring of his freshman year but pleaded with us during the summer to give him another chance. I remember his saying, "I think I can work harder."

Well, he did what he said he would. He worked harder. A lot harder. We red-shirted him in 1981, and he gained size and strength. He played a little as a sophomore in 1982 and even more as a junior, starting at tight end at 210 pounds, which is small (most tight ends are 220–240 pounds) but not impossible for one who puts in the kind of effort Brian did.

Another important factor in personal development is *perseverance*. Often in major college football the race doesn't go to the swiftest but rather to the one who is the most persistent and the most determined in his pursuit of a spot on the team. We consistently see players who come in as freshmen with less ability than other players but who eventually earn more playing time than their more talented teammates. Terry Luck was an athlete who showed unusual perseverance.

Terry enrolled at Nebraska in the early 1970s and was an outstanding quarterback on our freshman team. He looked like an almost certain three-year starter as he had size, speed, leadership, and could throw well. Then he suffered a freak knee injury in spring football and underwent surgery. He developed an infection, and this led to two more surgeries over the next two years. During this time, he couldn't play but worked hard at rehabilitation. Eventually he was able to come back for his senior year as the starting quarterback and team captain. He was replaced by Vince Ferragamo early in the year, again due to injury, and played sparingly the rest of the season. He went to the Cleveland Browns the next year and thought he had made the team, only to be released in the final cut. He went back the next year and finally made the team, a real triumph of perseverance in view of the difficulties he had overcome. We hope the perseverance one might learn in attempting to be a football player will carry over into other areas of life.

Still another area of personal development is the *broadening experience* that we hope a player might undergo during his years at the university. Acquiring an education opens new horizons. Certainly the travel and experience of playing football is broadening, and yet there is a danger many times that if athletes focus so exclusively on the weight room, the practice field, and athletic development they will become one-dimensional.

It's our hope that experiences as athletes and students will cause our players to be multi-dimensional people—people who are more flexible. Athletic ability is like money. It can be good or it can be bad depending on how you relate to it. The critical issue is whether you use *it* or it uses *you*.

Monte Johnson, who played for us in the early seventies and some years after that with the Oakland Raiders, believes we need to deprogram professional athletes, and he works to help them with their transition. Many former pros have a self-image problem after their athletic careers are over because they allowed athletics to use them rather than to view athletics as a means to an end. They did nothing to prepare themselves for life after sports participation—no reading, no off-season employment that would build a second career.

I believe Randy Gradishar of the Denver Broncos was the most thorough I've seen in preparing for life after professional football. Randy visited with anyone and everyone about their jobs and how to prepare for them. Randy recognized that after years of being treated as someone special, he was going to have to fend for himself in a new job market, and he prepared for this change much more rationally than anybody I've known.

The last important area in personal development is added *spiritual awareness* or *commitment*. Again, not all players make significant progress in this area, and some actually regress to being less committed than when they came to school. However, as a person struggles to become a better athlete and encounters disappointments and struggles in academic pursuits as well, he approaches the limits of his capability. Many times he will begin to realize his own resources are limited, and he will begin to rely more upon God's grace and attempt to be more committed spiritually. Some of the most satisfying points of my coaching career have come when I have observed very real and dramatic changes in the spiritual lives of players who had previously shown little spiritual depth.

I think of Turner Gill and Craig Sundberg, whom I've mentioned, who were solid and maturing in their faith while at Nebraska. But I have just as much pleasure in recalling Tony Davis, one of our outstanding running backs in the mid-seventies who, by his own admission, was something of a rowdy off the field. He called after my heart surgery to wish me well and said during the conversation, "I felt like I got my feet on the ground spiritually while I was at Nebraska, and it's really helped me and my family." His spiritual turnaround came after leaving Nebraska, but the seed may have been planted in our program.

Brett Moritz is a similar case. He came to Nebraska after being released from West Point. He got involved with the wrong crowd at Nebraska and never realized his full potential, but was nevertheless drafted very high by the NFL. He struggled to live up to his high draft and tussled with drugs and other problems off the field before straightening out his life spiritually. Eventually he joined the staff of the Fellowship of Christian Athletes in Florida. We were privileged to have Brett lead our chapel service before the 1984 Orange Bowl. It was hard to believe this was the same guy who had played for us only a few years earlier.

The effect of the overall football program doesn't end with the development of just the players themselves. The program also influences lives of countless young people who merely observe the program.

One of the most discouraging aspects of our society today is that there are so few positive role models with whom our young people might identify. As we watch television, go to the movies, or read the papers, we see entertainers, athletes, politicians, and public figures who don't represent all that they should. We talk to our players a good deal about the fact that participation in athletics is not a right but a privilege, and that with privilege goes responsibility.

The influence our athletes have can be used in a very positive or very negative way. For the most part, our players have a feeling of responsibility to young people and do a good deal of appearing and speaking at youth banquets, midget football banquets, and church affairs. This is very gratifying. On the other hand, occasionally we have situations come up where our athletes act in irresponsible ways, and this is very disappointing. Unfortunately, these negative occurrences generally receive much more publicity than the constructive things they do.

There are two statements I've heard that pretty well represent the two opposing philosophical views of athletics. The first, written by sportswriter Grantland Rice (I can remember first seeing this statement inscribed on a plaque on the wall of my great-uncle's office when I was only nine or ten years old): "For when the one Great Scorer comes to write against your name, it matters not that you won or lost, but how you played the game."

Obviously Grantland Rice was emphasizing the importance of the *process* of athletics—what we as athletes, coaches, and fans *become* in the process of athletic competition. He was saying that the end result—the final score, the outcome—is of only secondary importance.

On the other hand, many have heard another philosophy that is so often used in athletics: "Winning isn't everything, it's the *only* thing." This statement is diametrically opposed to that expressed by Rice, for it would indicate that the important thing about athletics is not so much the process or the "becoming" that goes on, but rather the end result. This type of reasoning often leads to the belief that the end justifies the means, resulting in much of the cheating and other seamy things we see in athletics today.

In a practical sense, winning is rewarded—sometimes financially, sometimes in praise and prestige, sometimes in contract extensions. And in most ways losing is punished—often in financial ways, often in firings, often in negative press. Therefore, regardless of what we might advocate, in an actual sense the philosophy our culture tends to embrace is "Winning isn't everything, it's the only thing."

Shortly after our 1984 loss to Oklahoma, an acquaintance approached me before a breakfast I have early each Thursday morning during the season in Omaha. The loss had knocked us from the number one spot in the polls, and I could see he was upset.

"What did you mean," he challenged, "when you said after the Oklahoma game that we tried not to put too much emphasis on winning? Some of us up here are really die-hard fans," he continued, "and it really bothers us when we hear statements about winning not being important."

I could tell from the way he said this that he was hoping I would try to amplify what I meant in my public remarks that morning. Apparently many Nebraska fans had been concerned we might have lost the game because winning wasn't very important to me.

What I was trying to convey following the Oklahoma game was that what we really emphasize with our players is *how* they play the game—the process of preparation, the effort they display during the game, the attitude they carry on the field. These are all things that we can control and that reflect on the process of athletics. Many times the end result—the win or the loss—we cannot control. It may hinge on the bounce of the football, it may depend on who has the better athletes, it may depend on an official's call. Therefore, we spend a lot more time trying to talk about process rather than end results with our players.

As a matter of fact, I can't recall ever telling the players we needed to win a given game. Rather, when we break our approach down in terms of the things we need to do well—such as avoid penalties, block downfield, concentrate in the kicking game, pursue well, tackle well— the players get a handle on what they're to do. When a coach gets emotional and starts yelling at players to go out and "win," many times it doesn't translate into effective action. It simply causes them to get emotional and engage in behavior that isn't well-directed.

Just as it's important to have a philosophy of athletics and a philosophy of coaching, it's also important to have a philosophy of offense and a philosophy of defense. Our offensive philosophy hinges on ball control. We want to have our offense on the field most of the time, and we believe that if we can initiate approximately eighty offensive plays a game while our opponents are initiating about sixty to sixty-five snaps a game, we'll have the best chance to win. We attempt to achieve ball control by doing everything we can to eliminate mistakes such as interceptions, turnovers, and penalties. We also believe the best way for us to control the football is to have a very strong running game. Therefore, we spend a large percentage of our practice time with our offensive line coming off the football blocking for the run, and we emphasize with our backs the need to run hard. We also believe in a very good passing game, but most of our passes are play-action passes that come off running plays and help complement the running game. Our passing game is designed to be a high-percentage type of passing that lends itself to the overall goal of ball control.

Defensively, our philosophy is that of being an attacking team, forcing the action rather than just sitting back and reacting to what the opponent does. We want to continually control the line of scrimmage, to stuff the opponents' blockers, to restrict running lanes, and to first of all stop the run. We would like to force our opponents to throw, and then, of course, we want great pursuit to the football. We want to force turnovers. Ideally, we would like to create three to four turnovers a game defensively and limit ourselves to none or one per game on offense. We feel the most important statistic in any football game is the turnover margin.

Unfortunately, what you *want* to have happen and what actually *does* happen isn't always the same, so much of our practice time and much of our discussion with players revolves around our philosophy of how to approach the game both offensively and defensively. If players don't have a clear idea of our philosophy, then, when things begin to go badly, they engage in a lot of random behavior that's not very productive.

It's no different with life. A purposeful philosophy can give life direction and productivity too.

Chapter Twenty-One

A Difficult Road to Walk

U ntil 1957, much of what I believed about God was a sort of second-hand religion. It was what my parents had professed, what I'd been told I *ought* to believe. I'd gone to church, gone to Sunday school, and was what folks would call a "religious person."

But it disturbed me that Christianity often was a pale experience for me. I sat in church with a lot of people who didn't seem to me to be very excited about what was going on. Christianity lacked reality and vitality in my life. Between my sophomore and junior years in college, however, I went to a Fellowship of Christian Athletes Conference at Estes Park, Colorado. I drove myself out there in my 1955 Plymouth not knowing what to expect. I really didn't know why I was going, except that I seemed to be searching for something. When I arrived at Association Camp outside Estes Park, located at the foot of the Rocky Mountains and the gate of Rocky Mountain National Park, I felt confused. Registration amidst hundreds of strangers. Assigned to a dorm room with strangers. Grouped in a huddle with more strangers.

But out of this confusion came a sorting out of life that has had a permanent impact on me.

It had been hard for me to believe that athletes—young aggressive people—would be attracted to Christianity. My Christian models often had been elderly and not very enthusiastic.

So the FCA conference was an eye-opener when I saw in person major college athletes I had only read about before. Ironically, there were ten or fifteen players from the University of Oklahoma whom I knew and admired. Clendon Thomas, Oklahoma's All-American halfback, was the leader of the ten or twelve young men in my huddle group.

SMU's Don Meredith was there. Jerry Stovall and a number of other players were there from LSU, which had a great football team at that time. Doak Walker was there. Olympian Bob Richards put on a pole-vaulting exhibition one night using the headlights of cars to see his way and a pit filled with sand to soften his fall. It was an impressive exhibition.

Adrian Burke, Otto Graham, and a number of other professional athletes were also there. I remember Dan Towler, Donn Moomaw, and Gary Demarest best. And these very impressive speakers spoke about their attempt to walk as Christians and how this Christian walk affected their athletic experience.

I returned from that conference more excited about Christianity. I had made an active, personal commitment. For the first time I had a true sense of where I was headed spiritually.

I went back to Hastings College enthused, but unfortunately I was the only person from Hastings at the conference. That fall, I went to the dorm to try to get some teammates involved in a Bible study, a sort of FCA huddle group experience. We met one or two times, but it seemed people just sat around and looked at me. They weren't too excited about what I was saying or what I wanted to have happen. The whole idea just kind of petered out.

It was disappointing to me. Here I was in a Christian college. I thought this kind of thing would really take off. But it didn't and it probably was because of my own inadequacy as well as the lack of interest on the part of those I was trying to reach. However, I was more successful teaching a senior high Sunday school class at my church.

The Estes Park experience was particularly important to me because I sensed a virility and vitality about Christianity—as well as a sense of warmth, a sense of acceptance and love. I had never experienced these before in any other environment including church, Sunday school, or other religious gatherings. The impact was deep and led to a personal commitment, a time when my faith really became my own and not a second-hand faith that somebody else wanted me to have.

Dag Hammarskjöld, in his book *Markings,* said he didn't really know the place or the time, but at some point in his life he said "yes" to life and made a spiritual commitment. That's the way that conference was for me. I can't pinpoint an exact moment, a particular Scripture verse, or a certain speaker, but the overall conference made an impact on me that truly started me on my spiritual journey that continues until this day.

I have found the athletic life on all levels to be challenging to that journey.

When I was involved with pro football, there were no chapel services before games (most teams now have them). Redskin's quarterback Norman Snead and I would quite often try to go to church on Sunday mornings if we could find one close. I tried to work at it myself, but the general atmosphere in pro football at that time was rather amoral and certainly not conducive to a strong spiritual life.

Coaching, too, has presented a variety of bumps and turns for my spiritual journey. The aspect of the job that has challenged my Christian walk most is the temptation to put other things before my faith. One of the biggest temptations is to make winning or being successful "in the world's eyes" more important than anything else. This can mean that much of my time and energy, everything about me, gets consumed in the business of trying to win.

Everyone is given some talent and a station in life, whether it's janitor, football coach, or president of the United States. Whatever it might be, we're accountable for how we use our talents and our position. Therefore I feel a responsibility to try to honor God with whatever abilities I have and the position I've been given. I think I've been given a great deal. Therefore, out of gratitude, I've attempted to be open and fairly vocal about my faith.

On the other hand, I've never felt it was my place or responsibility to preach to players or to try to convert them, to make them over in my image spiritually. Since to a large extent a coach holds the fate of his players' athletic careers in his hands, it would be very easy for him to abuse his position by trying to force his beliefs on them. Doing so would make me uncomfortable.

Usually in a meeting or two early in the season, I've tried to let the players know how important I think the spiritual dimension of life is. I do this simply as someone advising them on how to prepare themselves not just for games and seasons but for the long haul throughout their lifetime. I say, "We want you to be good athletes, and we'll do everything we can to help you be the best football players you can be. But that's going to take, on your part, a three- or four-year commitment. It's also important to be well-rounded academically and get a college degree because this will serve you longer than football— throughout your life until retirement age and beyond. It's important to choose carefully the people with whom you associate, for they help shape the things you think about and understand, the quality of your life. And the most important quality of life is spirituality, for it affects your life forever."

Beyond this there's nothing I can say. What I *do* is more important. I try to exemplify a Christian walk as best as I can as I coach. If I failed at this but preached at the players, I would do more harm than good.

I don't use profanity. I try to avoid being negative and don't use hatred toward opponents as a motivational or coaching tool. Rather we talk a lot about respecting our opponents, not retaliating, and about controlling the environment of a game by our actions to make it as positive as we can.

Athletic contests are a time of stress, almost like going into battle, and I think many players appreciate a time apart where they can gather themselves to focus on their spiritual life and their relationship with the Lord. For these reasons, we have chapel services before each game. We never try to use prayer or religion in any way to make us benefit or to triumph over an opponent, other than whatever readiness this "gathering" time might give the players to go out and play the best they can.

Before each game we have a silent prayer with each player praying as he sees fit. After a game we all get down on one knee in the locker room to give thanks for safety and the privilege of playing.

Anytime we're away at a bowl site or other city on a Sunday or religious holiday, we see that church services are provided. Throughout the season, we never infringe on Sundays so the players are able to worship as they wish. We encourage them to attend services, Protestant, Catholic, or Jewish.

So without a lot of preaching the players are well aware of my spiritual stance. I hope they will see some things in me that would make Christianity attractive to them in the same way those athletes at Estes Park first made the faith appealing to me.

My primary goal in life is to *honor Him*. When I keep that objective uppermost in my priorities, I find that life has meaning, relationships are better, and life seems good. When the goal gets twisted to *honor me*, as it often does, whatever I do has a hollow ring to it; I begin to drift, and things no longer seem to fit.

I think most Nebraska fans are aware of my spiritual stance, and I think a good many approve of it. Some probably don't. I know one common complaint about me during my first four or five years as head coach was that I was too nice a guy. The old "Nice guys finish last" business. There was this perception that we couldn't beat Oklahoma or win a championship or whatever because I'm too nice. I think there's still some of that feeling in Nebraska—couldn't beat Miami in the Orange Bowl, can't win the national championship—and yet I think there's less of that as time has gone on and as we have had consistently successful football teams.

I don't see any incompatability between being a football coach and being a Christian. The number one thing a coach has to do is to be himself; and if you're a Christian, then you'd better try not to be a hypocritical Christian. You'd better be consistent throughout whatever you do. The worst thing a coach can do is profess to be a Christian and then be devious in recruiting, manipulative in relations with players, or substandard in his or her personal life.

It's a difficult road to walk! To be a professing Christian in the highly emotional up-and-down game of football has lots of snares for coaches. And it makes extra demands on players, too.

As I read what Christ represented, who He was and what He said, and as I review the letters of Paul, I see we're called to be the best we can be. We're called to honor and glorify God by our actions and our thoughts. Certainly, then, a person who has made a serious Christian commitment and feels gifted athletically will not let himself off the hook very easily. If he is attempting to honor God, he will try to develop his skills as much as he possibly can.

An athlete who is committed to honoring God in his play is also going to be somewhat less anxious than someone who is determined to honor himself. The spiritually committed player is apt to be more team-oriented. He will be less upset about spending time on the bench, will realize where he fits into the total scheme of things, will be more supportive of the people around him, and will be more positive toward his teammates, particularly if things aren't going well for himself personally.

People relate to life in one of two ways, "What's in it for me?" or "What can I contribute?"

Christ was a man for others and continues to call us today to ask, "What can I contribute to this situation, to this team, to this organization?" A great football team doesn't need to have all spiritually attuned players on it, of course; but to have a nucleus of key players who have that kind of attitude, who are rather selfless, who give 100 percent, is a leaven that can be very helpful.

A strong Christian commitment will, in almost all cases, make a person free to operate more fully and more effectively. Certainly in my own life as a coach I think Christianity makes me less fearful of failure. Fear is a tremendous detriment in coaching or any other endeavor. So many times coaches think of all the bad things that can happen. We fret about the reaction of the public if we lose. Pretty soon we get stilted in what we're doing as a coach.

But if my primary goal is to serve and honor God, I'm able to do what I think I need to do and then accept the consequences in relatively good grace by knowing I have served Him. Then I measure success by how faithful I've been in honoring and serving God, not by wins and losses. A very freeing attitude!

Epilogue

Honoring Him

J anuary 1984...

"We're receiving an awful lot of mail about it, Tom."

"Oh boy, I'll bet we are!" I responded to my secretary, Mary Lyn.

"No, Tom. It's not too bad. Most feel the gamble showed real courage."

The long distance telephone connection didn't conceal Mary Lyn's relief, nor my wife's either when I talked to her later. Both had been anxious about public reaction to our 31-30 Orange Bowl loss to Miami, the result of our failed attempt at a two-point conversion trying to win instead of going for the surer one-point kick to tie the game and preserve our number one ranking.

In the days just following the game, as I traveled to recruit and then to attend the American Football Coaches Convention in Dallas, people addressed me with sort of pained, sorrowful expressions and hushed voices—as if I were in mourning.

So close again, but so far, I suppose they were thinking. *Always a bridesmaid, never a bride!*

Many people thought the narrow miss of yet another national championship would be devastating to me personally. It wasn't.

The 1983 season leading up to the 1984 Orange Bowl began with a

44-6 win over defending national champion Penn State in the Kick-Off Classic. We scored the first three times we had the ball in avenging our only loss of 1982. The impressive win put us atop the national rankings.

Mike Rozier gained 191 yards and set Nebraska's career rushing record during our next game, a 56-20 victory over Wyoming. Then we scored twenty-one points in each quarter in beating Minnesota 84-13 in Minneapolis. There was criticism following the game that we had "run up the score." The criticism came from writers who read the score but hadn't seen the game. Minnesota gambled by blitzing their linebackers a great deal. When they guessed right, they stopped us for little gain. When they guessed wrong, we usually scored. I have never seen so many big plays in one game. Our substitute players played over half the game.

Next I was rewarded with my one hundredth career head coaching victory—a 42-14 win over UCLA, the same school we defeated in my first game as head coach in 1973.

A pretty easy 63-7 win over Syracuse preceded a really difficult 14-10 win at Oklahoma State.

As always, Missouri played us very tough the next week, but we prevailed 34-13. Quarterback Turner Gill was great, hitting 14 of 18 passing attempts for 151 yards.

Colorado played us very well for a half the next week, but our 14-12 half-time lead turned into a rout as we scored forty-eight points in the third quarter. I wish I had taped that half-time speech. It must have been one of my better efforts.

We fell behind early in the game for the fourth consecutive week at Kansas State but recovered for a 38-5 half-time lead and a 51-25 final. Mike Rozier gained 227 yards on 23 carries, going over four thousand yards rushing for his career. He gained 212 yards on 26 carries the next week and scored four touchdowns in our 72-29 win over Iowa State. This gave him forty-seven career touchdowns, surpassing Johnny Rodgers's record forty-five.

Mike had a third great game the next week in our 67-13 win over Kansas—285 rushing yards on thirty-one carries, and four more touchdowns. He gained 230 yards the first half! He broke Lydell Mitchell's NCAA record of twenty-six touchdowns rushing in a single season and set Big Eight and Nebraska records for rushing in one season: 1,943 yards.

A fourth consecutive week of Mike's rushing over two hundred yards was just a sidelight of our twelfth game of the season at Norman, Oklahoma. Cornerback Neil Harris knocked away a fourth-down pass in the end zone with thirty-two seconds left to preserve our twenty-two-game winning streak and our third-straight unbeaten Big Eight title.

Some folks think we've been unlucky against the Sooners, but they forget this game. Oklahoma had a second down and one yard to go at our one yard line in the final minutes of play when they were penalized back to the six and then sacked at the nine. After a running play for no gain, Harris broke up third and fourth down pass attempts. It was a great finish, and this time the breaks went our way, the final score being 28-21.

And it was on to Miami.

We weren't enamored with the choice of our Orange Bowl opponent, since Miami University was basically a home team. Most of the time a bowl game is played on a neutral site and both teams have traveled a long distance and are living in hotels, away from familiar surroundings. Normally a team is not playing on its home field.

However, playing Miami anywhere would have been difficult because they were a very good football team. They had lost one game early in the year, then won ten straight games, and they were the type of football team we knew we would have a hard time defeating. I knew going in it would be a close, hard-fought game. I thought it would be decided by a point or two either way.

I remember praying the afternoon of the game that we would play well and would honor God through our performance that evening. I prayed we would conduct ourselves and play in a way that would be pleasing to Him, just about the same prayer I often give at our weekly devotional service the morning of each game.

But I was especially aware of that prayer during the last few minutes of the Orange Bowl game as we were coming up the field, trailing 31-24, but driving with a sense of inevitability. I thought we would quite likely score, make the two-point conversion, win the game, and be the undisputed national champions.

We didn't make the two-point play, but as I reflected after the game, I felt our demeanor, the attitude of the players, and the courage they had shown really were superlative. I was disappointed, and yet it was certainly not a shattering experience.

It was a great football game. I was sorry for the players that it didn't result in a national championship. Yet I had a great deal of admiration for the way they played. I thought they represented college football well.

I was especially proud of our team in view of the fact that when we got behind 17-0, and as we trailed through most of the game, we continually fought back and never gave up. In the fourth quarter, we appeared to be the stronger team but simply failed—a very near miss—on a two-point pass play.

I was also particularly pleased with the way our players responded after the game. When you're winning, when you're 12-0 and rolling over one team after another, it's easy for players to say the right things, do the right things, and be team-oriented. But when you come to the end of what could have been a national championship season and lose in a very disappointing manner, it could be easy to react with bitterness and say bad things about teammates, the opposition, and the coaching. I thought our players handled defeat well. They kept it in proper perspective. They maintained their composure and their dignity, and I appreciated that.

I don't know if the decision to go for the win "showed courage," as many folks have said. We never considered *not* going for the win. Courage involves choice, and in calling the two-point play, I wasn't aware of choice. To play for the national championship, the Orange Bowl, and the ill-defined feeling among players and coaches that we might be regarded as one of the truly great teams of all time simply dictated that we go for the win.

One of our players was quoted after the game as saying, "We didn't start practicing twice a day in 95° weather last August to go for a tie on January 2." This pretty well reflected the attitude of our coaches and players.

I guess kicking the extra point and tying the game would have given us the national championship, but that wasn't our goal. Our goals were to prepare well, try hard, and be in a position to win each game.

To that extent, we achieved our goals in the Orange Bowl.

My prayer had been to honor God. Sometimes prayer is answered in unlikely ways. To some, our loss to Miami was simply a bitter, disappointing defeat. To others, including myself, the game was exciting, well-played, a credit to college football, and, I hope, within God's view of what football and the human spirit should be.